# IN OTHER WORDS

## A BEGINNING THESAURUS

Andrew Schiller
William A. Jenkins

Scott, Foresman and Company

Editorial Offices: Glenview, Illinois
Regional Sales Offices: Palo Alto, California •
Tucker, Georgia • Glenview, Illinois •
Oakland, New Jersey • Dallas, Texas

# CONTENTS

ISBN 0-673-12430-4

2345678910-KPH-8988878685848382

# INTRODUCTION

## how to use this book

# A BOOK FOR WRITERS

Della liked to read stories and poems. She liked to write them too. Della's uncle was also a writer. He often sent Della books he thought she would enjoy.

For Della's birthday, Uncle Hank sent her a book called a thesaurus. Della looked through it quickly. Then she wrote a thank-you note.

> 3 Hammond Way
> Pueblo, Colorado 81003
> May 22, 19___
>
> Dear Uncle Hank,
> Thank you for the interesting book. I've never seen one like it before. It has so many interesting words in it. I'm sure it will help me once I learn how to use it.
> You always send me such interesting presents. Thanks again.
> Love,
> Della

Can you find a word that Della used too often in her letter?

Uncle Hank wrote back to Della.

127 Cardinal Street
New York, New York 10036
June 2, 19—

Dear Della,
   I'm glad you like the thesaurus. I hope
you've had a chance to study it by now.
You will find that it is a collection of
synonyms and antonyms. A synonym is a
word that is close in meaning to another
word. An antonym is a word that means the
opposite of another word. That makes it a
valuable tool for writers.
   Your thesaurus can help you
   —avoid using the same words over
     and over
   —choose the exact words you need
   —build your vocabulary
   —add sparkle to your writing.
   For example, in your letter to me you
used the word <u>interesting</u> three times.
Look up the entry for <u>interesting</u> in your
thesaurus. The entry words are in
alphabetical order, as in a dictionary.
Now, can you find three synonyms for
interesting that say exactly what you
mean? Try it!

              Love,

              Uncle Hank

P.S. I'm enclosing two pages that tell
how to use your thesaurus.

This is a copy of page 84 in your thesaurus. I've written numbers next to things on that page. These things are important for you to know about. For the explanations, see the page at the right.

**F**

2 **find**

3 *Find* means come upon something that had been lost. Did you ever *find* the book you misplaced? *Have* you ever *found* a lost dog? *Find* also means come to know something you didn't know before. I *found* that the word was too hard. I tried to hide my brother's birthday present where he wouldn't *find* it.

1

4 discover

*Discover* means find something that has been there, but no one has known about before. An explorer *discovers* new lands. I *discovered* baby birds in a nest.

unearth
uncover
dig up

*Unearth, uncover,* and *dig up,* all mean bring to light something that may be unknown or lost or forgotten. A farmer's plow might *unearth* an Indian arrowhead. A police officer may *uncover* a secret plot to rob the bank. You may *dig up* an old hat in the attic to wear to a costume party. We *dug up* an old schoolbook my grandmother used.

locate

*Locate* means find the position or place of something. You *locate* the North Pole on a map or on a globe. We must *locate* a gas station. If I lose my friends' address, I'll never be able to *locate* them.

Ralph can **locate** the North Pole on a globe.

5 ANTONYMS: misplace, hide, lose

8

**fine**

Look up *little* and *thin.*
Look up antonyms of *large* and of *rough.*

6

**finish**

Look up *end* (v). 7
Look up antonyms of *start.*

**firm**

Look up *hard.*
Look up antonyms of *soft.*

84

6

**1** This long section is called an *entry.* It contains the entry word and its synonyms and antonyms.

**2** This is an *entry word.* Entry words are printed in heavy black type. They are listed in alphabetical order in your thesaurus.

**3** This is the *paragraph of explanation.* It is printed next to the entry word. This paragraph explains the meaning or meanings of the entry word. It includes a sample sentence which helps to make each meaning clear.

**4** The words in light type under the entry word are its *synonyms.* Synonyms are words that are close in meaning to the entry word. A paragraph of explanation appears next to each synonym.

**5** The words in color at the bottom of the entry are *antonyms.* Antonyms are words that mean the opposite of the entry word.

**6** Not all entry words are followed by synonyms and antonyms. Some entry words are followed by *cross-references.* A cross-reference directs you to another entry word that has the information you want. For example, you would turn to the entry words *hard* and *soft* to find synonyms for *firm.*

**7** Some entry words can be used in more than one way. A *word-use label* tells you which way an entry word is used. For example, *end* is used as a noun on page 74 and as a verb on page 75. The (v) tells you to look up the entry for *end* used as a verb. Other word-use labels are (adj) for adjective; (adv) for adverb; (n) for noun.

**8** Many entry words have *illustrations* with *captions* which help to explain the meanings of entry words and synonyms.

After reading Uncle Hank's letter, Della looked up *interesting* in her thesaurus. She found six synonyms. Turn to pages 124 and 125 to see what they were. Then Della rewrote her letter using three of these synonyms in place of *interesting*.

Thank you for the absorbing book. I've never seen one like it before. It certainly has a lot of exciting words in it. I know how to use a thesaurus now, and it really helps me with my writing.

You always send me such fascinating presents. Thanks again.

Which three synonyms for *interesting* did Della choose? Compare the new letter with the old one to find out.

As you see, the new letter is better because it uses three different words in place of *interesting*. These words tell exactly what Della meant.

Della used her thesaurus to help make herself a better writer. You can do the same. Take time to do the exercises and games that follow. They will help you get to know your thesaurus. Then you too can use your thesaurus to make yourself a better writer.

# THESAURUS EXERCISES

When you come to a new town you need friends to show you around. The three exercises that follow are like new friends. They will lead you through *In Other Words* and show you how to use it.

## I. Reviewing the Parts

This first exercise will lead you through the parts of a thesaurus entry. When you finish, you will be ready to practice finding synonyms, as Della did.

**Directions**   Answer the seven questions that follow. Look back at pages 6 and 7 if you need help.

A. What is the *entry word* on page 144?

B. Look up **go**. How many pages long is the entry for **go**?

C. Look up **noise**. How many *synonyms* are given for *noise*?

D. Look up **hurry**. How many *antonyms* are given for *hurry*?

E. Look up **warm**. You will find a *cross-reference*. What two words should you look up to find synonyms for *warm*?

F. Look up **fast**. You will find two entries. Look at the *word-use labels* next to the entry words. In what two ways can *fast* be used?

G. Look up **funny**. What two synonyms do the *illustrations* and *captions* help to explain?

## II. Choosing Synonyms

A synonym is a word that is close in meaning to another word—close but not exactly the same. *Chop* and *saw* are synonyms for *cut.* They are both close in meaning to *cut*—close but not exactly the same. You *chop* a tree with an axe, not a saw. You can't use *chop* and *saw* to mean exactly the same thing. You must choose between them when you write.

This exercise will give you practice in choosing the correct synonym.

**Directions**   Look up the three entry words that follow. They are in heavy black type. Read the explanation for each of the three synonyms in each sentence. Decide which synonym you would choose to complete each sentence and why.

**A. go**
  1. The sound of the siren (melted, disappeared, faded) away.
  2. Jenny likes to (travel, ramble, proceed) in the park.

**B. hot**
  1. Mike's (steaming, flushed, sizzling) face showed how embarrassed he felt.
  2. Just before the rainstorm, the afternoon was (torrid, tepid, sultry) and uncomfortable.

**C. pull**
  1. The campers quickly (dragged, hauled, drew) their little canoe out of the water.
  2. The driver was (towing, hauling, tugging) an old car to the dump.

saw

chop

## III. Choosing Antonyms

An antonym is a word that means the opposite of another word. For example, *shady* and *dark* are antonyms of *bright.* They both mean the opposite of *bright.* But *shady* and *dark* do not mean exactly the same thing. A shady place is surrounded by light. A dark place has little or no light. You must choose between the two words when you write.

This exercise will give you practice in choosing the correct antonym.

**Directions**   Read the five sentences which follow. Look up the entry for each word in heavy black type. (If the entry has a cross-reference, look up the new entry as directed.) Look at the antonyms. Decide which antonym you would choose to complete each sentence and why.

**A.** Yesterday I was **sad** but today I am _____ .

**B.** The old road is **rough** but the new road is _____ .

**C.** This chicken is **stuffed** with rice but that one is _____ .

**D.** My math problems are **hard** but yours are _____ .

**E.** You **pull** on the door and I'll _____ .

shady

# THESAURUS GAMES

You know how to use your thesaurus. Now you can have some fun with it. Play the four games that follow. Each one is a plan for writing. You may use these plans in writing compositions, stories, and reports for class. They will make writing more fun.

## I. The Good Game: Using Adjectives

Remember how Della used her thesaurus to improve her letter to Uncle Hank? She found the words to say exactly what she meant.

dark

In the months that followed, Della continued to use her thesaurus. Soon she was watching and listening closely to her own words. She learned that she was using the same words over and over.

*Good,* for instance. Movies were good. People were good. Food was good. Records were good. Della was using *good* to describe everything she liked.

"It sounds as if everything I like is the same, and it isn't," she thought.

So Della looked up **good** in her thesaurus and made a list of synonyms. Then she made a list of things she liked and matched each thing with the synonym that best described how she felt about it.

"It's astonishing," Della wrote to Uncle Hank. "I learned dozens of new words. I also learned exactly how I really feel about all the different things I like!"

Della called this the Good Game. Now that you know how to use your thesaurus you can play the Good Game, too. Follow these steps.

## Directions

1. List 20 items—people, places, things—that you like.

2. Look up **good** and read the entry. Pay special attention to the last paragraph on page 101.

3. Find the synonym that best describes exactly what you like about each item on your list. Write the synonym next to the item. (See the example below.)

4. Write a sentence or two for each item. Be sure the sentences explain *why* you feel the way you do. Here is an example from Della's list:

My uncle Hank — considerate
My uncle Hank is a considerate person. He thinks about what other people need.

## II. The Action Game: Using Verbs

Della had to write a report for English class. Her father had just run in a six-mile race and had told her all about it. Now she was going to write the report from her notes.

"Wait," she said to herself. "The only action words in my notes are *run* and *jump.* I must find more action words or my report will sound dull."

So Della made lists of things her father had to jump over and the different speeds at which he ran during the race. She left a blank space before each item for each new action word.

Different words for **jump**

1. _____ a ditch
2. _____ a board fence
3. _____ a stream
4. _____ over a river by jumping from rock to rock
5. _____ a fallen tree

Different words for **run**
1. _____ slowly at the start
2. _____ with easy, steady strides while crossing a field
3. _____ faster while passing other runners
4. _____ as fast as he could while trying to catch other runners near the end of the race
5. _____ as fast as possible for the last 100 yards

Then Della looked up **jump** and **run** in her thesaurus. She read the entries carefully and chose her synonyms. She filled in each blank with the synonym that described exactly how her father jumped or ran. Della used her lists as an outline for writing her report.

Della called this the Action Game. You can play it, too. Follow these steps.

### Directions

1. Copy Della's lists on a piece of paper. Be sure to leave blank spaces for the new action synonyms.

14

**2.** Look up **jump** and **run** and read the entries carefully.

**3.** Find the best action synonym for each item on the lists. Write the synonym next to the item.

**4.** Write a sentence for each item. Be sure each sentence uses the action synonym to tell exactly what Della's father did.

## III. The How Game: Using Adverbs

Della wrote a composition about a visit with her Uncle Hank. Della's English teacher, Mrs. Barnes, wanted Della to rewrite it. Della had told what Uncle Hank looked like but not how he acted. What kind of person was he? Happy or sad? Quiet or loud? Did he do things quickly or slowly?

"You must use more adverbs in your paper," Mrs. Barnes said. "Adverbs tell *how* people act. Adverbs bring people to life on paper."

So Della went straight to her thesaurus and looked up **happy**. Uncle Hank was the happiest person she knew. Right away Della noticed that she would have to add *-y, -ly,* or *-ily* to the synonyms to make them into adverbs.

Turn to **happy** in your thesaurus to see what Della did.

First, Della had to turn the entry word **happy** into an adverb. That meant dropping the *-y* and adding *-ily: happily. Cheerful* was easier. She just added *-ly: cheerfully. Jolly* and *satisfied* just didn't sound right as adverbs so she left them off her list.

Then Della looked up **quiet** (adj). Uncle Hank had a quiet way of doing things as well as a quiet voice. Della found that she could turn all the words but *subdued* and *still* into adverbs she might use.

Finally, Uncle Hank was a fast person. There were two entries for **fast**. The second one—**fast** (adv)—had the adverbs listed already.

Della now had lists of adverbs for **happy, quiet,** and **fast**. Next, she made a list of things she could remember Uncle Hank doing. Della then matched each thing with the one synonym of **happy, quiet,** or **fast** that best described it. Finally, she made sentences from her list and used them in her new composition. Here are some examples from Della's list.

eats — rapidly    Uncle Hank always eats rapidly.
smiles — cheerfully   He smiles cheerfully when he sees me.
speaks — calmly    Uncle Hank speaks calmly.

Della called this the How Game. Here's how you play it.

### Directions

1. Turn to **brave** and read the entry carefully.

2. Make a list of adverbs from **brave** and its five synonyms. (Note: add -*ally* to *heroic*.)

3. Choose a brave person or animal, or make one up. List ten brave deeds that this person or animal did.

4. Match each deed with one of the six **brave** adverbs.

5. Turn each item in 4 into a sentence that tells about the brave deed and uses the adverb.

## IV. The Set Game: Using Nouns

Della's neighbor, José, had a problem. Something was wrong with his story for English class. He didn't like it, but he didn't know why. So he gave it to Della to read.

José's story was about a trip around the world. Della saw what was wrong with it.

"I like the story but it's not exact enough."

"Exact?" José asked.

"Look, the nouns are all the same. For example, you say that your hero flew in all kinds of aircraft. What kinds? Balloons? Jets? Gliders?"

José saw that Della was right. He had done the same thing for the animals, boats, and bodies of water in his story. José had written things like

—a bunch of lions
—a big boat
—a whole lot of water.

"What can I do?" he asked. "I don't know what you call a bunch of lions. I can't think of the word for the big boat."

"Here," said Della. "Look in my thesaurus." Della showed José part 3 of her thesaurus: *Sets*. Jose read page 222 to find out what sets were.

Turn to page 222 and read about sets. Then look through the rest of part 3.

Can you see why José should look at this last part of *In Other Words*?

"Oh — a *pride* of lions," José said, looking at page 226. "Thank you, Della. This thesaurus is terrific!"

Before long José had all the words he needed. He got them by playing the Set Game. Here's how.

### Directions

**1.** Make headings for 3 different lists:

<u>Places</u>          <u>Boats, Planes, Trains</u>          <u>Animals</u>

**2.** Pretend that you are taking a long trip. Look through part 3 of *In Other Words.* Fill in your lists with items from part 3. (Note: for *Places,* look at *Bodies of Water* and *Land Shapes.*)

**3.** Write a story about your trip. Use the words from your lists.

## USING YOUR THESAURUS

Remember to use your thesaurus for letters, reports, stories — anything you write. Play the thesaurus games. They will help you to pick the exact adjectives, verbs, adverbs, and nouns you need to make your writing sparkle!

# ENTRIES

a collection of entry words,
their synonyms and antonyms

**A**

about

*About* is an easy word to use if you are not sure just when something will happen or when it has happened. You might say you are *about* ready to go to school, or that it is *about* time to leave the party. You have supper *about* six o'clock every day. You saw a good TV show *about* a week ago.

Use the word *about* also when you are not sure how much or how many of something. I drank *about* a quart of milk. That tree must be *about* a hundred years old. Just *about* everyone went to the game. You may know someone who seems to be *about* seven feet tall. Some dogs look as if they are *about* six feet long.

You can use *about* to tell how far away something is. The airport is *about* five miles from here. I walked *about* a mile down the road.

almost
nearly

*Almost* or *nearly* might be used if you mean not quite. *Almost* everyone was laughing. I *almost* won the race. The show was *nearly* over by the time we got to the theater. It was *nearly* dark when they got home.

**Almost** everyone was laughing.

approximately

*Approximately* is a good word to use if you don't know whether something is a little more or a little less. It will cost *approximately* ten dollars to fix my bike. (It may cost seven dollars or twelve dollars.) My watch is *approximately* right. (It may be a minute fast or a minute slow.) You wouldn't say that *approximately* everyone was laughing, because there couldn't be more than everyone. You could say that it would cost *almost* or *nearly* ten dollars to fix the bike. But then you would mean it might cost eight or nine but not more than ten dollars.

Jason was **well-nigh** exhausted after running home.

practically
virtually
well-nigh

*Practically*, *virtually*, and *well-nigh*, all may be used to mean something so nearly true that the difference doesn't matter. You may be *practically* certain of something. A job may be *virtually* impossible to do. You may be *well-nigh* exhausted after running home.

ANTONYMS: precisely, exactly

**absorbing**     Look up *interesting*.

**ache**     Look up *hurt*.

**add**     Look up *say*.

**admire**     Look up *like*.
**affection**     Look up *love* (n).

# A

"I'm **afraid** I don't understand what you mean," Glen said.

**afraid**

*Afraid* means feeling fear. You might feel fear when a certain thing happens or is about to happen. We were *afraid* when we saw a storm coming. Or you might always feel fear of something. All my life I have been *afraid* of the dark. Many people are *afraid* of thunder and lightning.

The word *afraid* can be used in many ways. If you are just a little worried about something, not really feeling much fear, you might say you are *afraid* you'll miss the bus or you are *afraid* it's getting late.

Very often *afraid* is used in conversation without meaning that you feel fear at all. "I'm *afraid* you can't come in right now." "I'm *afraid* I don't understand what you mean." "I'm *afraid* you're wrong about that." This is just a polite way of saying, "You can't come in" or "I don't know what you're talking about" or "You're wrong."

There's one thing to notice about *afraid*. You can say a person or an animal is *afraid*, but you wouldn't say "That is an *afraid* person" or "The *afraid* cat ran away." The synonyms for *afraid* can be used both ways.

**timid**

*Timid* means shy and not willing to do anything daring or bold or dangerous. *Timid* people are not sure they can do or say the right thing. Alan was too *timid* to jump into the pool. The *timid* girl spoke so softly that no one could hear what she said. A *timid* person is not bold or confident.

frightened
scared

*Frightened* and *scared* are used when something has caused you to be afraid. The *frightened* cat seemed upset by the lightning. A *scared* rabbit can run very fast. Did you feel *scared* as you explored the cave?

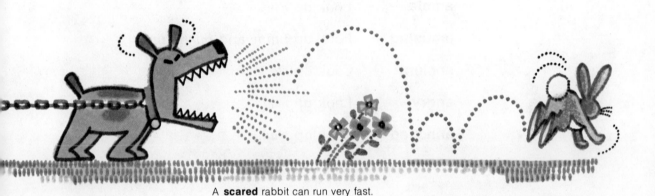

A **scared** rabbit can run very fast.

terrified

*Terrified* means shocked and trembling because something has suddenly made you very much afraid. A person who is usually unafraid might be *terrified* if a huge spaceship suddenly appeared overhead. You may be *terrified* if you see something that might hurt you. The *terrified* child began to scream when the lights went out.

ANTONYMS: daring, bold, confident, unafraid, fearless

| | |
|---|---|
| **aged** | Look up *old*. |
| **agree** | Look up *say*. |
| | Look up antonyms of *fight*. |
| **aid** | Look up *help*. |
| **alarm** | Look up *scare*. |
| **almost** | Look up *about*. |
| **alone** | Look up *lonely*. |
| **amble** | Look up *walk*. |
| **amusing** | Look up *funny* and *interesting*. |
| **ancient** | Look up *old*. |
| **angry** | Look up *mad*. |
| **annoyed** | Look up *mad*. |

People lived in caves in **ancient** times.

**answer** (n)  An *answer* is anything said or done because something is asked or done. You want to get an *answer* when you call someone on the telephone. When you write a letter to a friend, you look for an *answer*. You hope your *answer* to a math problem is correct. If you ask a question, you expect an *answer*.

reply  A *reply*, like an answer, tells you something you have asked or wondered about. When we asked to go to the movie, the *reply* was "No." I wrote to some museums asking about dinosaurs, and I have received three *replies*.

response  A *response* is an answer. Often it is not an answer in words. It is the way you act when something makes you feel glad or sad or angry or eager to do something. When Mr. Wu finished his speech, the *response* was a cheer from all of us. Bev's only *response* to the question was a laugh. There was no *response* when I knocked on the door.

retort  A *retort* is a quick, sharp answer. It may be clever or funny. Sometimes a *retort* is sharp and angry. "May we come in?" we asked Miss Jones. "No, you may not!" was her loud *retort*.

solution  A *solution* is the answer to some problem or puzzle. The mystery story was so puzzling that I didn't know until the last page what the *solution* was going to be. I finally found a *solution* to the problem.

ANTONYMS: question (n), problem

25

# A

**answer** (v)

*Answer* means speak or write or do something because someone asks or wants or needs something. When a person speaks to you, you *answer*. You *answer* a letter by writing to the person who sent it to you. If the doorbell rings, you *answer* by opening the door. You *answer* the phone by saying "Hello."

reply

*Reply* means answer. To *reply* to what someone says, you must think of what you are saying or doing. You usually *reply* with words. When Jay asked me to wait, I *replied* that I would. You can also *reply* with an action. When the band began its most famous song, the audience *replied* with shouts and cheers.

respond

You *respond* to something either by words or action. If a friend invites you to a party, you may *respond* eagerly, "I'd love to go!" If something or someone makes you happy, you may *respond* by jumping up and down. When a clown does a trick in the circus, people *respond* by laughing or clapping. Firefighters *respond* quickly when the fire alarm rings.

Firefighters **respond** quickly when the fire alarm rings.

retort

*Retort* means answer quickly and sharply. Sometimes a person *retorts* to an unkind or unpleasant remark with another. If someone tells you that your hair needs combing, you may *retort* angrily, "So does yours!"

solve

*Solve* means explain something that has been unknown or find the answer to a problem. We haven't *solved* all the problems of pollution yet. Do you think you can *solve* the match trick in ten minutes?

ANTONYMS: ask, question (v)

**Antique** cars are valuable.

**antique**       Look up *old*.

**appear**        Look up *come*.
                  Look up antonyms of *go*.

**approach**      Look up *come*.

**appropriate**   Look up *right*.

27

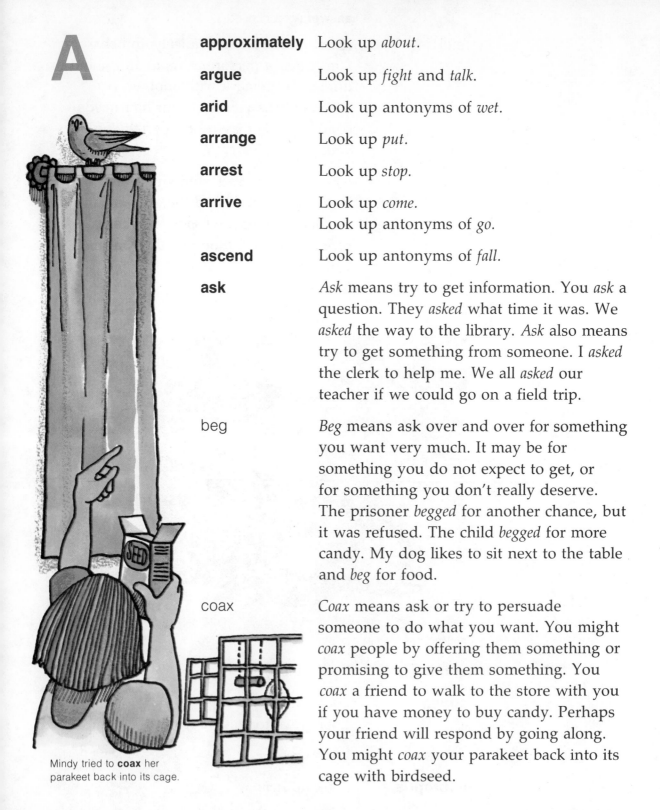

# A

**approximately**    Look up *about*.

**argue**    Look up *fight* and *talk*.

**arid**    Look up antonyms of *wet*.

**arrange**    Look up *put*.

**arrest**    Look up *stop*.

**arrive**    Look up *come*.
Look up antonyms of *go*.

**ascend**    Look up antonyms of *fall*.

**ask**    *Ask* means try to get information. You *ask* a question. They *asked* what time it was. We *asked* the way to the library. *Ask* also means try to get something from someone. I *asked* the clerk to help me. We all *asked* our teacher if we could go on a field trip.

beg    *Beg* means ask over and over for something you want very much. It may be for something you do not expect to get, or for something you don't really deserve. The prisoner *begged* for another chance, but it was refused. The child *begged* for more candy. My dog likes to sit next to the table and *beg* for food.

coax    *Coax* means ask or try to persuade someone to do what you want. You might *coax* people by offering them something or promising to give them something. You *coax* a friend to walk to the store with you if you have money to buy candy. Perhaps your friend will respond by going along. You might *coax* your parakeet back into its cage with birdseed.

Mindy tried to **coax** her parakeet back into its cage.

28

request        *Request* usually means ask for something or ask someone to do something. Our club will *request* an immediate report from the treasurer. We were *requested* to fasten our seat belts. We replied quickly by fastening them.

       *Inquire* means ask questions to find out about something. A stranger was *inquiring* about our neighbor's car. Some people came to *inquire* about the house for sale.

demand        *Demand* means ask for something that you mean to get. The robbers *demanded* money from the stagecoach passengers. He *demanded* an explanation when we were late. I *demanded* an apology, but she refused to give one.

       ANTONYMS: respond, reply (v), refuse, answer (v)

**assemble**     Look up *make*.

**assist**     Look up *help*.

**astonishing**     Look up *wonderful*.

The painting looked so real it was **astonishing**.

# A

**attend**     Look up *come.*

**attract**     Look up *pull.*

**attractive**     Look up *beautiful.*

**awful**     *Awful* is an overworked word. At first, *awful* meant full of awe, or awesome. Awe means great fear or wonder. An *awful* sight, or an awesome sight, filled people with fear and awe and wonder. For example, people who lived ages ago were filled with awe when they saw an eclipse of the sun. They thought that the world was coming to an end. Seeing a volcano erupt is an awesome or *awful* sight, even today.

But now people have changed the meaning of *awful.* They use it to describe a lot of things that other words could describe better. They use *awful* when they mean anything hard or unpleasant. It seems easier to use *awful* than to try to think of a

Seeing a volcano erupt is an awesome or **awful** sight, even today.

better word. Rainy weather is *awful*. A bad cold is *awful*. A hard arithmetic problem is *awful*. Here are some good words to use if you want to give poor old *awful* a rest.

horrible
terrible

*Horrible* and *terrible* mean very, very unpleasant and almost painful. I made a *horrible* mistake when I made a promise I couldn't keep. In the movie the *horrible* monster grabbed the dog. Sam took a *terrible* fall out of the apple tree. The nightmare was so *terrible* that I woke up screaming.

dreadful

When something seems dangerous or frightening, it is *dreadful*. It is a *dreadful* experience to be caught in a blinding snowstorm.

severe

*Severe* can mean causing great pain and trouble. A cold winter is *severe*. A *severe* toothache is no joke.

# B

**bad**

*Bad* is a word that describes anything that is not good. A careful writer tries to find other words that describe things more sharply and clearly.

naughty

*Naughty* describes little children who behave badly or do something bad that they know they shouldn't do. A *naughty* child may run and hide at bedtime. Taking a piece of candy after you are told not to would be *naughty*. Pets can be called *naughty* too.

harmful

*Harmful* describes something bad that might hurt someone or damage something. Staying out in the sun too long could be *harmful* to your health. Too much smoke in the air is *harmful* to a person's lungs. Washing clothes with very strong soap can be *harmful* to the cloth.

Washing clothes with very strong soap can be **harmful** to the cloth.

severe

*Severe* can describe something that is very bad because it is painful or hard to stand. A *severe* storm may cause damage to gardens and may flood streets and basements. A *severe* cold wave may cause plants to freeze. Someone with a *severe* illness may have to stay in bed a long time.

spoiled

*Spoiled* describes several things. *Spoiled* food is bad because it has been kept too long or has become too ripe. A *spoiled* child is used to having his or her own way about everything.

**Wrong** directions are worse than no directions at all.

poor  *Poor* can mean not as good as something could or should be. A *poor* movie may be badly made, or it may be boring. A *poor* throw in basketball probably would miss the basket. My teacher thinks my excuses for not doing my homework are *poor*.

wrong  *Wrong* means bad because it is not right. You can get lost if you go in the *wrong* direction. *Wrong* directions are worse than no directions at all. It's really bad to do something you know is *wrong*.

For other words you might be able to use instead of *bad*, look up *awful*, *careless*, *dangerous*, *dirty*, *sad*, *scary*. Also look up antonyms of *clean*, *great*, *kind*, *right*.

**bamboozle**  Look up *gyp*.

33

Pioneers **barred** the doors of their cabins.

| | |
|---|---|
| **bar** | Look up *shut*. |
| **battle** | Look up *fight*. |
| **beautiful** | *Beautiful* is the opposite of ugly. Anything that is very pleasing or delightful to look at or hear or touch is *beautiful*. You may speak of a *beautiful* baby or a *beautiful* sky or a *beautiful* fairy tale or *beautiful* manners. |
| pretty | *Pretty* is not as strong a word as *beautiful*. *Pretty* may describe someone who is pleasing to look at but not really *beautiful*. Someone who is lively, good-looking, or sweet is often referred to as *pretty*. Someone who is small and delicate may be called *pretty*. Things can also be described as *pretty*. |

You might speak of a *pretty* ring or a *pretty* dress or a *pretty* flower. A house may be painted a *pretty* color. A color that isn't *pretty* might be unattractive or ugly. A nice-looking girl is a *pretty* girl.

A bridge soaring across a river, a brilliant sunset, a snow-topped mountain, or a skyscraper would probably be called *beautiful*, not *pretty*.

A brilliant sunset would be called **beautiful.**

34

handsome

*Handsome* is used to describe someone, usually a man, who is pleasing to look at. *Handsome* is also used to describe an object, such as a building, that is well formed and pleasing to look at. The *handsome* old mansion looked dignified and stately in spite of the stores built up around it. The *handsome* horse looked almost like a statue. *Handsome* may be used to describe a woman who is good-looking in an unusual, noble way.

The **handsome** horse looked almost like a statue.

attractive

A pleasant sight that catches your eye may be called *attractive*. It attracts and pulls your attention. Juan has an *attractive* smile. A bowl of fresh flowers can make a table *attractive*. A bowl of wilted flowers would be unattractive.

lovely

*Lovely* describes something so beautiful that it makes you feel good to look at it or even think about it. Today is a *lovely* day for a hike in the woods. We have a *lovely* view of the lake. The garden looks *lovely*. Something the opposite of *lovely*—so ugly that it makes you feel shocked or bad to look at it—would be horrid or hideous.

Before you use the word *lovely*, though, look up the entry *lovely*. That entry may suggest some other words you'd rather use.

ANTONYMS: ugly, unattractive, horrid, hideous, plain, homely

**be fond of**

Look up *like*.
Look up antonyms of *hate*.

# B

Marvetta's dog likes to sit next to the table and **beg** for food.

**beg**       Look up *ask*.

**begin**     Look up *start* and *say*.
              Look up antonyms of *end* (v) and of *stop*.

**beginning** Look up antonyms of *end* (n).

**behold**    Look up *look*.

**believe**   Look up *think*.

**big**       When something is called *big*, it may be *big*
              in size or in importance. A *big* dog can
              jump over a fence easily, but a little dog
              can't. A *big* decision or a *big* problem is one
              that is very important and must be
              carefully thought about.

              You can picture a *big* mountain, a *big*
              crowd, a *big* ice-cream cone. But you know,
              of course, they are not all the same size.
              *Big* is a word that can be used to describe
              almost anything that is bigger than
              something else. Here are some other
              excellent words to use instead of *big*.

**big** continued

A mountain may be *immense* or *majestic*. An ocean is *vast*.

A crowd is often *huge, great, enormous,* or *tremendous.*

*Huge, gigantic, colossal, large,* all are good words to describe something that is very *big* in size.

A *big* city is *large* but it is also *important.*

Someone who is a *big* help on a project is *valuable* and quite often *necessary* or *essential.*

A *big* parade is usually *grand* or *magnificent, thrilling* or *exciting.*

A *big* athlete is *great, excellent, skilled.* He or she is *necessary* or *valuable* to the team or the school.

A *big* movie star is *famous* and *important.* Sometimes he or she is *great.*

Look up *large* and *great* and *important.*

Chiang is **valuable** to the team.

The giant standing in the path **blocked** their way.

| | |
|---|---|
| **bilk** | Look up *gyp*. |
| **blank** | Look up *empty*. |
| **blast off** | Look up *go*. |
| **bleak** | Look up *cold*. |
| **block** | Look up *shut*. |
| **boisterous** | Look up *loud*. Look up antonyms of *quiet* (adj). |
| **bold** | Look up *brave*. Look up antonyms of *afraid*. |
| **bolt** | Look up *run*. |
| **boring** | Look up antonyms of *funny* and of *interesting*. |
| **bound** | Look up *jump*. |
| **boundary** | Look up *end* (n). |

The deer **bounded** into the woods.

**brave**
*Brave* is the opposite of cowardly. *Brave* means able and ready to face danger. *Brave* soldiers may be afraid, but they still won't run. They are not cowardly.

bold
*Bold* means not only ready but eager to face danger. Lion tamers have to be *bold*. Timid people could not train wild animals.

courageous
*Courageous* means willing to face danger and do whatever you believe is right or is your duty. A *courageous* person refuses to do something that he or she believes is wrong. *Courageous* people are not afraid to say "No."

fearless
*Fearless* people are not fainthearted or shaken by danger. A firefighter who goes into a burning building to rescue someone is *fearless*, not cowardly.

gallant
heroic
*Gallant* and *heroic* mean brave and willing to fight whether you win or lose.

*Brave* and its synonyms can describe people and the things people do. Knights did many *brave* deeds. An adventure may be *bold*. A rescue is *courageous*. A speech can be *fearless*. Many *gallant* and *heroic* deeds are done by ordinary people.

ANTONYMS: cowardly, timid, fainthearted

Knights did many **brave** deeds.

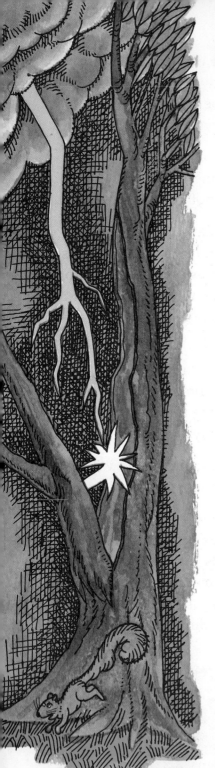

The huge tree **split** when it was struck by lightning.

**break**     *Break* means suddenly come apart or force something to come apart. Some dishes *break* if you drop them. A cook *breaks* an egg to open it. When a water pipe *breaks*, it must be repaired. I *broke* my arm when I fell off the swing. Phil *has broken* his pencil.

crack     *Crack* means break, but not into pieces. A stone may *crack* a window, but the glass will stay in one piece. A piece of wood can *crack* without falling apart. Be careful not to *crack* that plate.

shatter     *Shatter* means break into many small
smash     pieces. *Smash* means break by force, too, but not always into pieces. A driver who hits a tree might *shatter* or *smash* the windshield. The driver might *smash* a fender, but he or she would not *shatter* it.

crush     *Crush* means break into tiny pieces by grinding. People *crush* ice. Machines *crush* stones. *Crush* also means squeeze together or push into the ground. Kate *crushed* her hat when she sat on it. The dog *crushed* the flowers in our garden.

split     *Split* means break or cut from end to end or into layers. If you *split* a banana and put ice cream on it, what are you making? *Split* also means divide or separate into parts. The huge tree *split* when it was struck by lightning.

fracture     *Fracture* is often used to mean break a bone. If you fall out of a tree, you may *fracture* your leg. It may take several weeks for your leg to heal.

tear

*Tear* means break apart by pulling or yanking. You might *tear* your sleeve if it catches on a nail. If you *have torn* your sleeve, you can mend it with a needle and thread. If you *tore* a piece of paper, you could have fastened it together with tape.

A balloon **bursts** if too much air is blown into it.

burst
explode

*Burst* and *explode* mean break violently and sometimes noisily from a force inside. A balloon *bursts* if you blow too much air into it. Fireworks *explode*.

damage

*Damage* usually means hurt or break an object so that it is not as valuable or as useful as before. A severe windstorm may *damage* a house by blowing off its roof. If you *damage* a chair by breaking off one leg, the chair can usually be repaired or fixed.

demolish
destroy
wreck

*Demolish*, *destroy*, and *wreck* mean tear down or break so completely that an object cannot be fixed. The tornado *demolished* everything in its path. The waves *destroyed* our sand castle. Max *wrecked* his bike when he hit a tree.

Some of the synonyms for *break* can be used to describe other actions which have nothing to do with breaking. You might *burst* into a room to announce good news. Your neighbor might *explode* if you leave your skates on the stairs. Your team might have *smashed* the other team 14 to 0. Your hopes are sometimes *shattered*.

Look up *cut* for other words to use.

ANTONYMS: repair, heal, mend, fasten, fix

# B

**bright**

*Bright* is the opposite of dim. *Bright* means either sending out light, like the sun, or reflecting it, like the moon.

sunny

A *sunny* day is bright with sunshine. A cloudy day is gray and dark. A cloudy day could also be called dreary or gloomy.

shiny

An object is *shiny* when it has been cleaned and polished so that it reflects light. It is not dull or dingy.

brilliant

*Brilliant* means brighter than usual. The jewel looked *brilliant* against her dark gown. Stars look *brilliant* on a cold, clear night.

flashing
sparkling

*Flashing* and *sparkling* mean sending out quick bursts of light. A *flashing* light comes from just one place, like a turn signal on a car or the light on a fire truck. A *sparkling* light comes from different spots on a surface—like snow *sparkling* in the sunlight.

glistening
glittering

Say *glistening* and *glittering.* You'll hear that *glistening* sounds slippery, and *glittering* sounds hard and cold. A wet street or something covered with oil is *glistening.* Cold, bright stars at night or pieces of broken glass in the sunlight are *glittering.*

gleaming
glowing

*Gleaming* and *glowing* describe a steady light. A *gleaming* lantern shines through the darkness. A *glowing* fire makes a room warm and cozy. You can cook over *glowing* coals.

A wet street is **glistening.**

Car headlights are sometimes **glaring.**

dazzling
glaring

*Dazzling* and *glaring* mean bright enough to hurt the eyes. Sunlight on snow is *dazzling*. Car headlights are sometimes *glaring*.

light

*Light* is the opposite of dark. The sky may be *light* blue in the early morning and dark blue at night. A full, bright moon can make the night so *light* that you can see to read a book.

vivid

*Vivid* means bright because of strong color. New blue jeans have a *vivid* color. After many washings they look faded.

gay

*Gay* may mean cheerful and bright in color. The room was painted a *gay* pink. *Gay* may also mean bright and merry. The baby's eyes were dancing, and his laugh was *gay*.

See *smart* (adj) for more words that you could use. Also see the antonyms of *dim* and of *stupid*.

ANTONYMS: dim, dark, dreary, gloomy, dull, dingy, faded, shady

# B

Charlene's dog feels **bristly**.

| | |
|---|---|
| **brilliant** | Look up *bright* and *smart* (adj). Look up antonyms of *dim* and of *stupid*. |
| **bring** | Look up *carry*. |
| **bristly** | Look up *rough*. |
| **broad** | Look up antonyms of *thin*. |
| **buddy** | Look up *friend*. |
| **build** | Look up *make*. |
| **bulky** | Look up antonyms of *little* and of *thin*. |
| **bumpy** | Look up *rough*. Look up antonyms of *smooth*. |

Larry gets a **bumpy** ride when he drives on a **bumpy** road.

| | |
|---|---|
| **burning** | Look up *hot*. |
| **burst** | Look up *break*. |
| **bury** | Look up *hide*. |
| **buy** | Look up *get*. |

Mr. Howard stopped to **buy** food at the supermarket.

# C

| | |
|---|---|
| **call** | Look up *say* and *shout*. |
| **calm** (adj) | Look up antonyms of *mad* and of *excited*. Look up *quiet* (adj). |
| **calm** (v) | Look up antonyms of *scare*. |
| **capture** | Look up *catch*. |
| **careful** | Look up antonyms of *careless*. |
| **careless** | *Careless* means not careful. Some people are *careless* about hanging up their clothes. *Careless* people do not think or care about other people's things or even their own things. A *careless* boy may leave his bicycle somewhere, then go off and forget it. A *careless* girl may lose her lunch money on the way to school. A *careless* classmate may borrow your eraser, then forget to return it. |
| reckless | *Reckless* means getting into danger without thinking. A *reckless* bicycle rider does not obey traffic laws. Cautious riders do. |

Some people are **careless** about hanging up their clothes.

*This is sloppy Handwriting*

sloppy
: *Sloppy* can mean careless about how you look or how you do something. His clothes were wrinkled, and they looked *sloppy.*

hit-or-miss
: *Hit-or-miss* means not planning how you do something or not caring how well you have done it. A *hit-or-miss* job is one you hurry to finish. If you are painting a wall in a *hit-or-miss* way, your brush hits parts of the wall and misses parts, but you don't bother to go back and paint the places you missed.

thoughtless
: *Thoughtless* means not caring or thinking about what you are doing. It also means not caring about how others feel. Slamming the door when you know someone is sleeping nearby is a *thoughtless* thing to do. If you hurt a friend's feelings because you said something without thinking how it would sound, you were being *thoughtless.*

ANTONYMS: careful, cautious, thoughtful, watchful

# C

**carry**

*Carry* means hold something while you move. The cat *carried* her kitten across the street. Then she dropped it in the grass. The movers have *carried* all the funiture outside. Will they leave it there?

bring
take

You *bring* a package if you carry it from some other place to where you are now. You *take* a package if you carry it from where you are now to some other place. *Bring* your camping equipment to my house tonight, and I'll *take* it to school for you tomorrow. Bonnie *brought* hers, and I *took* it yesterday. Bill *has brought* his tent, but I *have* not *taken* it yet.

deliver

*Deliver* means bring or send to a person or place. When can you *deliver* the groceries we ordered? I have to get up early every morning to *deliver* papers.

transport

*Transport* means move or carry something or someone from one place to another. Buses *transport* passengers; trucks *transport* animals and objects. Before railroads were built, pioneers *transported* their families to the West in wagon trains.

Pioneers **transported** their families to the West in wagon trains.

fetch

*Fetch* means go and get. My dog *fetches* sticks when I throw them. Jack and Jill were supposed to *fetch* water from a well.

tote

*Tote* is used by people in some parts of the country to mean carry in your arms or on your shoulders or on your back. Students *tote* their books to school. Sailors *tote* their clothes in duffel bags.

Look up *send*. You may find more good words for what you want to say.

ANTONYMS: drop, leave, let go

**carve**

Look up *cut*.

**catch**

*Catch* means get or take hold of something that has been moving or hiding. You might *catch* a ball (if you don't miss), *catch* fish, *catch* a glimpse of someone. In olden days men *caught* animals for food. Explorers in many lands *have caught* strange animals.

*Catch on* and *catch up with* are idioms. When you understand the rules, you *catch on* to the way a game is played. If you hurry, you can *catch up with* someone ahead of you.

rope
net
trap

*Rope, net,* and *trap* mean catch an animal by getting it into something it can't get out of. A cowboy *ropes* a calf by throwing a loop around the calf's neck and pulling it tight. People *net* fish when they throw a big net into the water and then pull it back full of fish. You would *trap* mice with a mousetrap. *Trap* is often used to mean

**catch** continued on page 50 ▶

The pirates **captured** the ship.

**catch** continued from page 49

catch or stop a person or an animal. Police *trapped* the escaped tiger when it ran into a shed. We were *trapped* when the elevator stopped between floors. Rescuers had to come and free us.

snatch
grab
seize

*Snatch, grab,* and *seize* mean quickly and suddenly take hold of something. You might let go of it later. The monkey *snatched* the candy bar out of my hand. He wouldn't let go of it. The mountain climbers *grabbed* a rope when they felt themselves falling. The mail carrier *seized* the growling dog by the collar.

capture

*Capture* means catch or take by force. The pirates *captured* the ship and *seized* the crew. Later they released the crew.

See *get* for other words you might want to use.

ANTONYMS: miss, free, let go, release

| | |
|---|---|
| **cautious** | Look up antonyms of *careless*. |
| **cease** | Look up *stop*. |
| **chase** | Look up *run*. |
| **chat** | Look up *talk*. |
| **cheat** | Look up *gyp*. |
| **cheerful** | Look up *happy*.<br>Look up antonyms of *sad*. |
| **cheerless** | Look up *cold*. |
| **chilly** | Look up *cold*. |
| **chip** | Look up *cut*. |

Andy is trying to **pick out** the most exciting book he can find.

**choose**
*Choose* means decide to take or do something. You *choose* a library book that you want to read. You hope you *have chosen* a good book. Instead of taking the bus home from the library, you may *choose* to walk and refuse to ride. If it rains, you may be sorry you *chose* to walk.

pick
*Pick* means choose from many just what you want. When someone offers you jellybeans, perhaps you *pick* all the black ones. When two groups choose sides for a game, each captain tries to *pick* the best players.

*Pick out* is an idiom meaning choose carefully. The first person to get on a bus can *pick out* the best seat. You *pick out* the most exciting book you can find on the shelf.

*Pick on* is an idiom meaning annoy or tease one who can't fight back. A bully *picks on* smaller children.

**choose** continued on page 52 ▶

They looked at the candy and then **selected** the kinds they like best.

select    *Select* means choose and decide on after thinking carefully about reasons for taking one thing instead of another. Perhaps you look at the candy on the store counter and then *select* the kinds you like best. In a supermarket, shoppers *select* the ripest, reddest apples. When you buy a pair of shoes, you try on several before you *select* the pair you want and reject the others.

elect     *Elect* usually means choose one person over others by voting. To be *elected*, a person must receive more votes than all the others. The fourth grade will *elect* class officers today.

ANTONYMS: refuse, reject, leave

**52**

| | |
|---|---|
| **chop** | Look up *cut*. |
| **chuckle** | Look up *laugh*. |
| **chum** | Look up *friend*. |
| **clamor** | Look up *noise*. |
| **clean** | *Clean* is the opposite of dirty. A *clean* shirt is one that is new or that has been washed or that has no dirt or spot on it. |
| neat | *Neat* means clean. It also means in order or in place. A person's hair might be clean but mussed up and untidy. It is *neat* if it is clean and combed. |
| spotless<br>unspotted<br>unstained | *Spotless, unspotted,* and *unstained,* all mean without any dirt, spots, or stains. The windows were *spotless* after Gene washed them. |
| pure | *Pure* means perfectly clean or spotless. Something that is *pure* is not mixed with anything that would make it impure. Water is *pure* if it is not polluted by dirt or germs. *Pure* air becomes polluted when chimneys pour out smoke. |
| spick-and-span | You have a *spick-and-span* room if it has just been cleaned and tidied up. |
| | ANTONYMS: dirty, untidy, impure, polluted, unclean, soiled, filthy, grimy |
| **clear** | Look up antonyms of *dim*. |
| **clever** | Look up *smart* (adj).<br>Look up antonyms of *stupid*. |
| **clip** | Look up *cut*. |

Dog owners **clip** their dogs.

# C

**close**        Look up *end* (v) and *shut*.
Look up antonyms of *start*.

**clump**        Look up *walk*.

**coarse**        Look up *rough*.
Look up antonyms of *soft* and of *thin*.

**coax**        Look up *ask*.

**cold**        *Cold* is the opposite of hot. Something that is *cold* has a temperature lower than the temperature of your body. When you take a bottle of soda pop out of the refrigerator, it feels *cold*.

cool
chilly        If you feel *cool* or *chilly*, you feel not quite cold. *Cool* means pleasantly and comfortably cold. The *cool* breeze felt good after the sun went down. The weather was *cool* and rainy. You are probably not uncomfortable when it is *cool* outside.

*Chilly* is unpleasantly cold but not so cold that you can't stand it. The room became *chilly* when the fire died down. It was too *chilly* to go swimming. The difference between these two words is that it is pleasant to feel *cool*. It is not pleasant to feel *chilly*. Warm is their antonym.

frosty        Something is *frosty* if it is covered or looks as if it is covered with frost. Grass may be *frosty* on a cold autumn morning. When windows are *frosty*, you can't see through them.

Some rivers get **icy** in winter.

| | |
|---|---|
| icy | Something *icy* is covered with ice or filled with ice or feels like ice. A street may be *icy*. Some rivers get *icy* in winter. An *icy* wind makes you cold. |
| unfriendly | Cold may be the opposite of kind or friendly. Some people seem cold and *unfriendly* when you first meet them. |
| bleak cheerless | *Bleak* and *cheerless* mean cold, unfriendly, and unpleasant. The old house looked *bleak* on the cold, windswept hill. A bare room is *cheerless*. |

The other synonyms of *cold* may also be used to describe something or someone *unfriendly*. We received a *cool* welcome from our friends because we were so late. Rod's smile was *chilly*. Miss Brown gave me a *frosty* glance when I stepped in front of her.

ANTONYMS: hot, warm, kind, friendly, torrid, sweltering

55

A doghouse may **collapse** if it isn't built right.

**collapse**    Look up *fall*.

**colossal**    Look up *large*.

**come**    *Come* usually means move toward a speaker or an object, not away from. *Come* is the opposite of go. Your teacher may say "*Come* to school early tomorrow." Perhaps you *came* home late yesterday. Or you *had* just *come* into the room when the bell rang.

Some of the following words aren't really synonyms for *come*, but often they may be used in place of it when you want to show a special meaning.

arrive    *Arrive* means come to a certain place. It may be the end of a journey or trip. I hope you will *arrive* at my house before the others have to leave. The bus *arrived* at one o'clock and departed at two. After a long winter we were glad to see spring *arrive*.

enter

*Enter* can mean come into a place. You *enter* a building. In a play an actor *enters* when he or she comes onto the stage. We saw them when they *entered* the room. But they left before we had a chance to speak to them.

attend

*Attend* can mean come to or be present at something. Her great-grandmother *attended* a one-room school. Twelve people will *attend* our meeting. Only seven *attended* the last one.

approach

*Approach* means come near or toward something. Soon we'll *approach* a bend in the road. An airplane descends gradually and *approaches* the runway before it lands.

appear

*Appear* means come into sight. A person can *appear* at a window or around a corner. Boats *appear* over the horizon. Spots may *appear* on your body if you get the measles. They will disappear when you are well again. *Appear* can also mean seem to be. The instructor *appeared* timid as he stood up to speak. There *appears* to be no mistake in this letter.

A boat **appeared** over the horizon.

loom

*Loom* means come into sight or appear. But it often is used when something appears in dim or foggy light and looks larger than it really is. Suddenly, as we stumbled in the darkness, the tree *loomed* in front of us. The sailors were frightened when another ship *loomed* out of the fog right in front of them.

ANTONYMS: leave, depart, disappear, go

57

# C

Bob tried to **conceal** the kitten under his jacket.

| | |
|---|---|
| **comical** | Look up *funny*. |
| **comment** | Look up *say* and *talk*. |
| **common** | Look up antonyms of *queer*. |
| **commotion** | Look up *noise*. |
| **companion** | Look up *friend*. |
| **compel** | Look up *make*. |
| **complete** | Look up *end* (v). |
| **complicated** | Look up *hard*. |
| **comrade** | Look up *friend*. |
| **conceal** | Look up *hide*. Look up antonyms of *show*. |
| **conclude** | Look up *end* (v) and *stop*. Look up antonyms of *start*. |
| **conclusion** | Look up *end* (n). |
| **confident** | Look up antonyms of *afraid*. |
| **conserve** | Look up *keep*. |
| **consider** | Look up *think*. |
| **considerate** | Look up *kind*. |
| **construct** | Look up *make*. |
| **consume** | Look up *eat*. |
| **contented** | Look up *happy*. Look up antonyms of *sad*. |
| **continue** | Look up *say*. Look up antonyms of *stop*. |
| **cool** | Look up *cold*. Look up antonyms of *hot* and of *excited*. |

It didn't take long to **construct** this model airplane.

| | |
|---|---|
| **cooperate** | Look up *help*. |
| **correct** | Look up *right*. |
| **courageous** | Look up *brave*. |
| **cover** | Look up *hide*. |
| **cowardly** | Look up antonyms of *brave*. |
| **crack** | Look up *break*. |
| **crammed** | Look up *full*.<br>Look up antonyms of *empty*. |

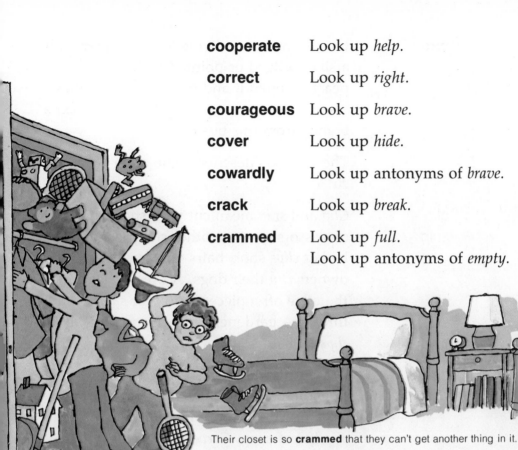

Their closet is so **crammed** that they can't get another thing in it.

| | |
|---|---|
| **cranky** | Look up *mad*. |
| **crazy** | Look up *mad* and *stupid*. |
| **creamy** | Look up *smooth*. |
| **create** | Look up *make* and *start*. |
| **cross** | Look up *mad*. |
| **crowded** | Look up *full*.<br>Look up antonyms of *empty*. |
| **cruel** | Look up antonyms of *kind*. |
| **cruise** (n) | Look up *trip* (n). |
| **cruise** (v) | Look up *go*. |
| **crush** | Look up *break*. |

# C

**cut**

*Cut* means open, divide, or take away with a sharp-edged or pointed tool. You *cut* a peach to open it and get the pit out. Nick *has cut* the pie into pieces. Yesterday I *cut* a branch from this bush.

These words describe some other ways to cut.

clip
snip

*Clip* and *snip* mean cut with short strokes of scissors or some other sharp edge. A barber *clips* short hairs off your neck. Dog owners *clip* their dogs. A dressmaker *snips* the edge off a piece of cloth or *snips* off a thread. A gardener *snips* off rosebuds, but *clips* a bush.

carve
slice

*Carve* can mean cut carefully to form something. An artist *carves* a figure from a piece of wood. You might *carve* a rose out of a bar of soap. *Carve* and *slice* also mean cut by moving a knife back and forth through something. You *carve* meat when you cut it in pieces for serving. You *slice* bread or meat when you cut thin, flat pieces from a loaf or a roast.

slit

You have *slit* a board if you have cut it lengthwise or in long, thin pieces. The tailor *slit* cloth when he made a long cut in it. To open a letter you *slit* the envelope along the fold at the top.

slash

*Slash* means make heavy, deep cuts without being careful where you cut. Explorers *slash* through a jungle when they swing heavy, sharp knives against the vines and underbrush.

Explorers **slash** through a jungle.

Lynnette **chops** wood with an ax.

peel　　　You *peel* potatoes or apples when you cut away the skins.

saw　　　You *saw* a piece of wood by cutting it with back-and-forth strokes of a sharp saw. We *sawed* logs for the fireplace.

chip　　　You *chip* a piece of ice or a rock if you cut off small pieces from the edges. Meg *chipped* the stone until it fit into the hole.

chop　　　*Chop* means cut in pieces with many short, hard blows—a person *chops* wood with an ax. Cooks *chop* vegetables.

You may find other words for what you want to say if you look up *break*.

**cute**　　　*Cute* is a tired word. People use it too often. Before using *cute*, look up some of these other words to see if you can find one that fits better!

A *cute* puppy might be *naughty, friendly, comical*.

A *cute* baby may be *beautiful, attractive, bright*, or *happy*.

A *cute* trick may be *clever* or *unusual* or *funny*.

A *cute* movie might be *amusing, interesting, entertaining, hilarious*, or just *pleasant*.

A *cute* boy or girl is probably *attractive, thoughtful, friendly*, and not ugly or unpleasant, cross or irritable.

A *cute* sweater may be *attractive, pretty, bright*, or *dainty*.

# D

| | |
|---|---|
| **dainty** | Look up antonyms of *rough*. |
| **damage** | Look up *hurt* and *break*. |
| **damp** | Look up *wet*. |
| **dangerous** | *Dangerous* means likely to cause injury or harm or loss unless great care is taken. Riding a bicycle on a dark street may be *dangerous*. An escaped lion is *dangerous*. |
| unsafe | *Unsafe* means not free from danger or from the risk of injury. Thin ice is *unsafe* for skating. A leaky boat is *unsafe*. A bicycle with bad brakes is *unsafe*. |
| risky<br>hazardous<br>precarious | *Risky*, *hazardous*, and *precarious*, all mean something is uncertain because there is a chance of danger. If you haven't had measles, it would be *risky* to visit someone who has them. Icy sidewalks make walking *hazardous*. You could find yourself in a *precarious* position if you climbed a tall tree and then couldn't get down. |

A leaky boat is **unsafe.**

ANTONYMS: safe, harmless

| | |
|---|---|
| **daring** | Look up antonyms of *afraid*. |
| **dark** | Look up *dim*.<br>Look up antonyms of *bright*. |
| **dart** | Look up *fly*. |
| **dash** | Look up *hurry*. |
| **dawdle** | Look up antonyms of *hurry*. |
| **dazzling** | Look up *bright*.<br>Look up antonyms of *dim*. |
| **deceive** | Look up *gyp*. |

62

| | |
|---|---|
| **declare** | Look up *say*. |
| **deliberate** | Look up antonyms of *fast* (adj). |
| **deliberately** | Look up antonyms of *fast* (adv). |
| **delicate** | Look up antonyms of *rough*. |
| **delighted** | Look up *happy*.<br>Look up antonyms of *sad*. |
| **delightful** | Look up *wonderful*. |
| **deliver** | Look up *carry*. |
| **demand** | Look up *ask*. |
| **demolish** | Look up *break*.<br>Look up antonyms of *make*. |
| **demonstrate** | Look up *show*. |
| **depart** | Look up *go*.<br>Look up antonyms of *come*. |
| **deposit** | Look up *put*. |
| **descend** | Look up *fall*. |
| **deserted** | Look up *empty*. |
| **desolate** | Look up *lonely*. |
| **despise** | Look up *hate*. |
| **destroy** | Look up *break*.<br>Look up antonyms of *make*. |
| **detest** | Look up *hate*. |
| **devotion** | Look up *love* (n). |
| **devour** | Look up *eat*. |

Deep-sea divers might **descend** to the bottom of the ocean.

# D

**difficult**     Look up *hard.*

**dig up**     Look up *find.*

**dim**     *Dim* can be the opposite of bright. The light inside a cave is *dim*. An object or a thought or a sound that is not clear may also be called *dim*. You might have only a *dim* idea of how a machine works. A voice can sound *dim* and far away.

dull     *Dull* means not clear or not shining and bright. You might think that gray is a *dull* color and orange is a gay color. Bright red is vivid. On a *dull* day the sky is cloudy. If the sun suddenly comes out, it may be dazzling. Thunder booming in the distance makes a *dull* sound.

shady
shadowy
dark     *Shady, shadowy,* and *dark* mean that some of the light has been cut down or cut off in some way. The willow tree gave us a *shady* place to eat our lunch. As we sat around the campfire after supper, Robin noticed two *shadowy* figures come out of the forest and walk toward us. When the moon went behind a cloud, the night was *dark*.

smoky
misty     *Smoky* and *misty* are often used to describe air that is not clear. The air gets *smoky* when people burn leaves. The air is *misty* near a waterfall. We carried flashlights through the *misty* night so that we could find our cabin.

foggy     *Foggy* describes air so full of mist you can hardly see through it. We went through the *foggy* streets without even seeing the

Some people **dig up** old hats to wear to a costume party.

64

people ahead of us. You might also use *foggy* to mean that your thoughts are mixed up or not clear. Dee was still a little *foggy* about following the directions we gave her.

The farmer dressed the scarecrow in an old **faded** suit.

| | |
|---|---|
| gloomy | *Gloomy* means dim and dark and cheerless. The room looked *gloomy* when all the windows were shut and the shades were pulled down. |
| faded | When something has become less bright and less colorful than it was, it is *faded*. We dressed the scarecrow in an old *faded* suit and a tattered hat. |
| muffled<br>faint | *Muffled* and *faint* describe sound that has been softened or deadened in some way. The *muffled* voices coming from behind the closed door sounded angry. The *faint* sound of music came through the open window. *Faint* also describes a sight or thought that is not clear or plain. The *faint* outline of a mountain in the distance told the sailors they were nearing the shore. I had only a *faint* idea of what the word meant. |

See the antonyms of *bright* for other words you might want to use.

ANTONYMS: bright, clear, gay, vivid, dazzling, brilliant, radiant, glowing, shiny, gleaming

**dim-witted**  Look up *stupid*.
Look up antonyms of *smart* (adj).

**din**  Look up *noise*.

# D

**dingy**    Look up *dirty*.
             Look up antonyms of *bright*.

**direct**   Look up *show*.

**dirty**    *Dirty* is the opposite of clean or pure. Your clothes sometimes get *dirty* when you play outdoors.

soiled       *Soiled* means dirty because of being worn or used too long without being washed. A shirt or a dress that has been worn for several days becomes *soiled*. Sometimes clothes that have been tried on by many shoppers look *soiled* before anyone buys them.

Roger had a **stained** tongue from eating blueberries.

spotted      *Spotted* and *stained* mean unclean because
stained      something has been put on or spilled on clothing or some other item. Your clothes may be *spotted* if an ice-cream cone drips on them. Roger had a *stained* tongue from eating blueberries.

filthy       *Filthy* and *grimy* are stronger words
grimy        meaning very dirty. A house that is not cleaned for a long time will probably become *filthy*. The baby's clothes were *filthy* after he had played in the mud. We peeked through the *grimy* window of the deserted barn.

smeared      *Smeared* and *smudged* often mean dirty
smudged      because of careless handling. A wall is *smeared* if someone has touched the paint before it is dry. If you spill a drop of paint or ink on a picture and then try to rub it off, the whole thing may look

*smeared.* If your hands are very dirty when you write, your paper will probably be *smudged.*

dingy

*Dingy* means dirty and without brightness or color. The trapper lived in a *dingy* cabin. The house looked *dingy* until we painted it. If you mix watercolors and get too much black or brown in, you may end up with a *dingy* gray.

impure
polluted

*Impure* and *polluted* mean not clean or pure because dirt or other materials are in something. It is dangerous to drink water that may be *impure.* Rivers and lakes are often *polluted* because garbage is dumped in the water.

ANTONYMS: clean, pure, spick-and-span, unspotted

**disagree**      Look up *fight.*

**disagreeable**  Look up *mad.*

**disappear**     Look up *go.*
                  Look up antonyms of *come.*

A magician makes objects seem to **disappear.**

# D

| | |
|---|---|
| **discard** | Look up antonyms of *keep*. |
| **disclose** | Look up antonyms of *hide*. |
| **discontinue** | Look up *stop*. |
| **discover** | Look up *find*.<br>Look up antonyms of *hide*. |

Claudia **discovered** baby birds in a nest.

| | |
|---|---|
| **discuss** | Look up *talk*. |
| **disgruntled** | Look up *mad*. |
| **disguise** | Look up *hide*. |
| **dislike** | Look up *hate*.<br>Look up antonyms of *like*. |
| **dispatch** | Look up *send*. |
| **display** | Look up *show*. |
| **dispute** | Look up *fight* and *talk*. |

| | |
|---|---|
| **dive** | Look up *jump*. |
| **downcast** | Look up *sad*.<br>Look up antonyms of *happy*. |
| **drag** | Look up *pull*.<br>Look up antonyms of *push*. |
| **draw** | Look up *pull*. |
| **dreadful** | Look up *awful*. |
| **dreary** | Look up antonyms of *bright*. |
| **drenched** | Look up *wet*. |
| **drive** | Look up *push*. |
| **drop** | Look up *fall* and *end* (v).<br>Look up antonyms of *carry*. |
| **dry** | Look up antonyms of *wet*. |
| **dull** | Look up *dim* and *stupid*.<br>Look up antonyms of *bright*, of *smart* (adj),<br>of *interesting*, and of *funny*. |
| **dumb** | Look up *quiet* (adj) and *stupid*.<br>Look up antonyms of *smart* (adj). |

Jackie **dived** into the pool.

# E

**eager**    Look up *excited*.

**earn**    Look up *get*.

**easy**    Look up antonyms of *hard*.

**eat**    *Eat* means put in the mouth, chew, and swallow. We *eat* breakfast early. We *ate* outside yesterday. Do you know anyone who *has eaten* bear meat? *Eat* can also mean destroy by wearing away or taking away a little at a time. A strong acid will *eat* through something it has been spilled on. A river can *eat,* or wear away, its banks and form a canyon.

consume    *Consume* means eat or use up a large amount. A crowd at a ball game can *consume* hundreds of hot dogs. *Consume* can also mean destroy. The fire *consumed* the log.

devour    *Devour* means eat greedily. A hungry lion in the zoo *devours* the meat. If you were so hungry that you *devoured* five doughnuts, you would have stuffed them into your mouth and eaten them as fast as you could. If you were so hungry that you *consumed* five doughnuts, you would have eaten them all, but we wouldn't know how fast you had eaten them.

Many different words may be used to describe how animals eat. We use some of these same words to tell how people eat.

feed    Horses *feed* on hay and grain. Some large fish *feed* on smaller fish. Cows that *have fed* in a cornfield may become sick.

Horses **feed** on hay and grain.

graze
: Cows and horses in a pasture *graze* when they bite off and eat grass. In summer flocks of sheep *graze* on the mountainside.

gnaw
: When a dog *gnaws* a bone, it wears away the bone by biting on it for a long time. Because this meat is so tough, I have been *gnawing* one piece for five minutes.

nibble
: A rabbit *nibbles* a lettuce leaf when it eats small bits at a time. The girl sat and *nibbled* her apple.

gobble
: *Gobble* means eat fast and greedily. If you are hungry enough to eat five doughnuts, you may *gobble* the first one, but when you come to the last one, you will probably *nibble* it.

gulp
: *Gulp* means drink in large swallows or swallow food without stopping to chew. The child *gulped* two pieces of candy before anyone noticed.

If Sam is hungry enough to eat five doughnuts, he might **gobble** the first one.

But when he comes to the last one, he will probably **nibble** it.

The fourth grade will **elect** class officers today.

**elderly**    Look up *old*.

**elect**    Look up *choose*.

**empty**    *Empty* is the opposite of full. *Empty* means having nothing inside. Something may be *empty* because what it usually contains is not there. An *empty* house has no furniture or people in it. An *empty* desk has nothing in its drawers. An *empty* gas tank has no gas in it. You may have an *empty* feeling by evening if you forget to eat some lunch.

vacant    *Vacant* means empty. A *vacant* house is not occupied. It has no people living in it, though it may have furniture. A *vacant* chair is one with nobody sitting in it. A *vacant* lot has no buildings on it.

If you sit staring into space with your thoughts far away, you might be accused of having a *vacant* stare.

deserted

*Deserted* can mean left empty and uncared for. A *deserted* house is empty when the people who lived there have moved away and no one else wants to move in. *Deserted* houses often look run-down.

blank

*Blank* usually describes a surface that is empty because it has nothing on it. A *blank* page in a book has no writing on it. A *blank* space in a test is a place for an answer. A person who starts to say something and suddenly forgets what it is might explain that his or her mind suddenly went *blank*.

hollow

*Hollow* means empty or having a hole inside. A *hollow* tree is one in which the inside has rotted away, leaving the trunk empty. A garden hose is a *hollow* tube. A soda straw is *hollow*.

ANTONYMS: full, occupied, crammed, crowded, packed

**encourage**    Look up *push* and *help*.

A **hollow** tree is one in which the inside has rotted away, leaving the trunk empty.

# E

**end** (n)
An *end* means the very last point to which something can go.

limit
A *limit* is a point that you can not or may not go beyond—a speed *limit,* a time *limit.*

boundary
A *boundary* usually is a line that marks the end or limits of a piece of land. Fences often mark the *boundaries* of yards.

tip
The *tip* is the end of something long and slim—the *tip* of a finger or of a pencil.

conclusion
The *conclusion* is the end of something that has been done or has happened. We read the *conclusion* of the story.

finale
A *finale* is usually the end of a musical piece or the last part of a stage performance. The *finale* was loud, with trumpets blaring and drums thundering. Everyone in the show took part in the *finale.*

outcome
result
An *outcome* or a *result* is what happens at the end of something you do or hope for or work for. The *outcome* of the story was that the tortoise won the race. We had good *results* when we made cookies.

The **outcome** of the story was that the tortoise won the race.

goal
A *goal* is an end or result that you work for. Pam's *goal* is to be a singer.

purpose
A *purpose* is like a goal but usually means a reason for doing something. Jim's *purpose* in writing the note was to ask for help.

ANTONYMS: beginning, outset

**end** (v)

Mrs. Lopez **closes** her popcorn stand every fall.

To *end* means the opposite of to start or begin. It means quit doing something or come to the point where there is no more. The game *ended* in a tie.

finish
complete
conclude

*Finish, complete,* and *conclude,* all mean bring to the end whatever you have started to do. You *finish* a puzzle when you put the last piece in place. Plumbers *complete* a job when they do all the things they were hired to do. A doctor *concludes* a checkup when he or she has done everything necessary to find out if the patient is healthy. *Conclude* can also mean come to an end. You might say, "The book *concludes* with an exciting rescue scene." But you wouldn't say a book *finishes* or *completes* with a rescue scene.

close

*Close* means end something by limiting the time. Mrs. Lopez *closes* her popcorn stand every fall. She will open it again in May.

stop

*Stop* means end suddenly what you are doing, whether it is finished or not. You *stop* a game you have just started when you are called to supper. You *stop* writing when you have *finished* a story.

drop

*Drop* can mean end something suddenly. You end an argument when you *drop* the subject and introduce a new one. The art project was *dropped* when we ran out of paint.

Look up *stop* for other words to use.

ANTONYMS: start, begin, open, introduce, launch

# E

| | |
|---|---|
| **enemy** | Look up antonyms of *friend*. |
| **enjoy** | Look up *like*.<br>Look up antonyms of *hate*. |
| **enjoyable** | Look up *wonderful*. |
| **enormous** | Look up *large*. |
| **enraged** | Look up *mad*. |
| **enter** | Look up *come*. |
| **entertaining** | Look up *funny* and *interesting*. |
| **enthusiastic** | Look up *excited*. |
| **escape** | Look up *go*. |
| **essential** | Look up *important*. |
| **establish** | Look up *make* and *start*. |
| **even** | Look up *smooth*. |
| **exactly** | Look up antonyms of *about*. |
| **examine** | Look up *look*. |
| **exasperated** | Look up *mad*. |
| **excellent** | Look up *good*. |

Dr. Moy **examined** Fred's throat.

**excited**     *Excited* can be the opposite of quiet. *Excited* means feeling strongly about something and showing your feelings. You may be indifferent to something that you don't feel *excited* about. When you are *excited*, you may feel either good or bad. You are *excited* about having a vacation. In an argument you might get *excited* when you should keep cool. You'd be pretty *excited* if a fire engine stopped in front of your house. You might look calm, though.

eager     *Eager* means wanting to do a certain thing or being very much interested in something. Everyone is *eager* to go to the party. *Eager* faces appeared as the plate of cookies was passed around.

impatient     *Impatient* means excited and unwilling to wait for something. Waiting for the rain to stop made us *impatient*. Some people are very *impatient* if they have to wait in line.

enthusiastic     *Enthusiastic* means eager and excited about something. The class was *enthusiastic* about the new project and couldn't wait to start.

ANTONYMS: quiet (adj), indifferent, cool, calm (adj)

**exciting**     Look up *interesting*.

**exclaim**     Look up *say*.

**excursion**     Look up *trip* (n).

**exhibit**     Look up *show*.

**expedition**     Look up *trip* (n).

**explode**     Look up *break*.

Fireworks **explode**.

**fabulous**    Look up *wonderful*.

**fade**    Look up *go*.

**faded**    Look up *dim*.
Look up antonyms of *bright*.

**faint**    Look up *dim*.

**fainthearted**    Look up antonyms of *brave*.

**fair**    Look up *right*.

**fall**    *Fall* means move downward or become less or lower. Some leaves *fall* in autumn. Last night the temperature *fell* below zero. It began to rise this morning. After the flood the river *had fallen*.

drop    *Drop* means fall swiftly or unexpectedly or let something fall. Some money *dropped* out of the hole in my pocket. I was carrying so many papers that I *dropped* some of them. You also can *drop* your voice to a whisper or *drop* your eyes by looking down or *drop* off to sleep.

sink    *Sink* means fall or become lower, sometimes slowly. A stone *sinks* when it falls to the bottom of a lake. The sun appears to *sink* as it sets. The boat *sank* slowly. Some boats *have sunk* fast.

The sun appears to **sink** as it sets.

descend    *Descend* can mean move lower or go downward. Planes *descend* before they land. When they take off, they ascend. Deep-sea divers might *descend* to the bottom of the ocean. The path *descends* sharply to the river. The princess *descended* the stairs slowly.

tumble    *Tumble* means fall suddenly, maybe rolling over and over. A person climbing a tree may slip from a branch and *tumble* to the ground.

topple    *Topple* means fall because of too much weight on top or because of being off balance. If you stack boxes too high, they will *topple*. The chimney was so tall that people were afraid it would *topple* when a strong wind blew.

collapse    *Collapse* means fall apart or cave in. After a hundred years the old barn *collapsed*. Something you are building or putting together may *collapse* if the job is not done right.

ANTONYMS: rise, ascend

Chief Joseph was a **famous** leader of the Nez Percé Indians.

**false**    Look up antonyms of *right*.

**famous**    Look up *important*.

**fascinating**    Look up *interesting*.

**fashion**    Look up *make*.

# F

A **fast** runner can get to home plate safely.

**fast** (adj)     *Fast* is the opposite of slow. As an adjective, *fast* means able to move from one place or position to another in a very short time. A *fast* runner can get to home plate safely.

rapid     *Rapid* means fast in movement. A *rapid* river flows fast. A sluggish river moves slowly.

swift     *Swift* means fast or happening suddenly. Pete took a *swift* look around the room. We had a *swift* change of plans.

speedy     *Speedy* means able to move rapidly or to get something done very fast. The *speedy* clerk was back with our package before we knew it. A poky clerk makes everyone wait. You would speak of a river as *rapid* or *swift*. You would not call it *speedy*.

quick     *Quick* means fast in learning or understanding or doing something. Liz gave a *quick* answer to the question. Roy was *quick* to understand and do the work.

hasty     *Hasty* means in a hurry and perhaps too fast to be carefully thought out. A *hasty* decision may not be as good as a more deliberate one.

sudden
instant     *Sudden* and *instant* mean happening or acting very fast. These are the opposite of gradual. If you call your dog, it may come to a *sudden* stop. You can make *instant* pudding in a very short time.

ANTONYMS: slow (adj), sluggish, poky, deliberate, gradual, unhurried

**fast** (adv)  As an adverb, *fast* tells how something or someone moves. One child ran *fast*. The others walked slowly. My watch was running *fast*, not slow. The synonyms for the adverb *fast* have the same meanings as the synonyms for the adjective *fast*.

rapidly
swiftly
speedily
quickly
hastily
suddenly
instantly

The river runs *rapidly* or *swiftly*, not sluggishly. Get your work done *speedily*. Then we can go swimming. Tina decided *quickly* or *hastily*, not deliberately. The cat gradually got closer to Fran. Then it *suddenly* leaped onto her lap. José dropped the hot pan *instantly*.

*Fast* can also mean tightly when it tells how you do something. Hold *fast* to the rope. Tie the boat *fast* to the dock so that the boat won't float away.

Fran's cat **suddenly** leaped onto her lap.

If you are not quite sure why *fast* is used both as an adjective and as an adverb, this may help. The adjective tells <u>what kind</u> of person or thing you are describing. For example, a person may be a *fast* or a *swift* runner. The adverb tells <u>how</u> someone or some thing does something. You'd say that person ran *fast* or *swiftly*.

ANTONYMS: slowly, slow (adv), sluggishly, deliberately, gradually

**fasten**  Look up antonyms of *break*.

**fat**  Look up antonyms of *thin*.

**fearless**  Look up *brave*.
Look up antonyms of *afraid*.

**feeble**  Look up antonyms of *strong*.

81

# F

**feed**      Look up *eat*.

**fetch**     Look up *carry* and *get*.

**feud**      Look up *fight*.

**fiery**     Look up *hot*.

Steel in a blast furnace is **fiery**.

**fight**    *Fight* means struggle against someone or something. People may *fight* by hitting each other, or they may *fight* with words. Sometimes students *fight* on the playground. Medicine *fights* infection. The plane *fought* head winds all the way. Many soldiers *have fought* in two wars.

disagree    When people *disagree*, they have different ideas. The girls agreed to have a party but *disagreed* on what day to have it.

argue    *Argue* means offer reasons for your point of view. Two people who disagree on something may *argue* all day and still not change each other's mind. You can *disagree* with someone without *arguing*.

dispute

*Dispute* means argue angrily or question what someone thinks. Joy told her brother that eight o'clock was his bedtime, but he *disputed* her right to tell him when to go to bed.

squabble
quarrel

*Squabble* and *quarrel* mean argue noisily. The children *squabbled* over who should go first. It is not a good idea to *quarrel* with your neighbors.

quibble

*Quibble* means argue about something that is not very important. The two girls were *quibbling* over whether the glass was half full or half empty.

The two girls were **quibbling** over whether the glass was half full or half empty.

feud

*Feud* means quarrel with another family or group for a long time. The two families *feuded* over the boundaries of their farms for many years.

oppose

*Oppose* means be against or object to something. It is stronger than disagree. I *oppose* the plan to charge thirty cents to get into the children's zoo.

battle
war

*Battle* and *war* mean fight or struggle violently. The swimmers had to *battle* the waves. You *battled* a cold all winter. The police *war* against crime constantly.

ANTONYM: agree

**filthy**

Look up *dirty*.
Look up antonyms of *clean*.

**finale**

Look up *end* (n).

# F

**find**

*Find* means come upon something that had been lost. Did you ever *find* the book you misplaced? *Have* you ever *found* a lost dog? *Find* also means come to know something you didn't know before. I *found* that the word was too hard. I tried to hide my brother's birthday present where he wouldn't *find* it.

**discover**

*Discover* means find something that has been there, but no one has known about before. An explorer *discovers* new lands. I *discovered* baby birds in a nest.

**unearth**
**uncover**
**dig up**

*Unearth, uncover,* and *dig up,* all mean bring to light something that may be unknown or lost or forgotten. A farmer's plow might *unearth* an Indian arrowhead. A police officer may *uncover* a secret plot to rob the bank. You may *dig up* an old hat in the attic to wear to a costume party. We *dug up* an old schoolbook my grandmother used.

**locate**

*Locate* means find the position or place of something. You *locate* the North Pole on a map or on a globe. We must *locate* a gas station. If I lose my friends' address, I'll never be able to *locate* them.

ANTONYMS: misplace, hide, lose

Ralph can **locate** the North Pole on a globe.

**fine**

Look up *little* and *thin.*
Look up antonyms of *large* and of *rough.*

**finish**

Look up *end* (v).
Look up antonyms of *start.*

**firm**

Look up *hard.*
Look up antonyms of *soft.*

| | |
|---|---|
| **fit to be tied** | Look up *mad*. |
| **fix** | Look up antonyms of *break*. |
| **flashing** | Look up *bright*. |
| **flat** | Look up *smooth*. |
| **flee** | Look up *run*. |
| **fleecy** | Look up *soft*. |
| **flight** | Look up *trip* (n). |
| **flimsy** | Look up antonyms of *strong*. |
| **fling** | Look up *throw*. |

Because Bonita made mistakes while writing a letter, she crumpled the papers and began to **fling** them at the wastebasket.

| | |
|---|---|
| **flit** | Look up *fly*. |
| **float** | Look up *fly*. |
| **fluffy** | Look up *soft*. |
| **flurry** | Look up *noise*. |
| **flushed** | Look up *hot*. |
| **flutter** | Look up *fly*. |

# F

**fly**

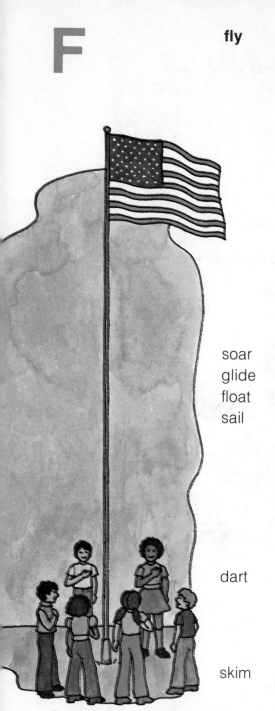

The flag **is flown** at school.

soar
glide
float
sail

dart

skim

*Fly* means move through the air with the help of wings. Birds and airplanes *fly*. Birds *flew* south last fall. They *have flown* over our house every year. *Fly* also means make something move through the air. Pilots *fly* airplanes. Many people like to *fly* kites. We *fly* our flag on the Fourth of July. But *fly* can also mean move fast and easily. Louis *flew* to answer the doorbell. The days *fly* by. The boat seemed to *fly* over the water.

We use many other words to mean move swiftly or easily, even though they are not synonyms of *fly*.

*Soar, glide, float,* and *sail,* all mean move easily. A bird *soars* when it flies upward in the sky. A baseball *soars* when it is hit over the fence. A bird can *glide* through the air without moving its wings. An ice skater seems to *glide* over the ice. *Float* and *sail* mean move on the surface, but we say clouds *float* across the sky or the ball *sailed* over the fence. Cinderella seemed to *float* down the stairs.

*Dart* means move quickly from place to place. A hummingbird *darts* from flower to flower. A rabbit may *dart* from a hollow log and disappear down a hole.

*Skim* means move quickly just above or on a surface. A low-flying plane *skims* over the trees. A sailboat *skims* over the water.

flutter
flit

*Flutter* and *flit* mean move quickly from one place to another, sometimes with nervous, jerky motions. Leaves *flutter* to the ground. A scrap of paper seems to *flutter* along the street on a windy day. A hungry bird *flitted* from branch to branch. Some children *flit* from one toy to another.

hover

*Hover* means hang in the air almost without moving. A sea bird *hovers* in the air until it sees a fish in the water below. Then it dives to catch the fish. Helicopters can *hover* over the ground.

*Fly* also means escape or run away. By the time the sheriff's posse arrived, the bank robbers *had flown* to the hills.

See *go* and *hurry* for other words to use.

Helicopters can **hover** over the ground.

Sometimes they have to **force** their friend to take a bath.

| | |
|---|---|
| **foe** | Look up antonyms of *friend*. |
| **foggy** | Look up *dim*. |
| **fondness** | Look up *love* (n). |
| **fond of** | Look up *like*.<br>Look up antonyms of *hate*. |
| **foolish** | Look up *stupid*. |
| **force** | Look up *make*. |
| **forceful** | Look up *strong*. |
| **forlorn** | Look up *lonely* and *sad*. |
| **form** | Look up *make*. |
| **fracture** | Look up *break*. |
| **frail** | Look up antonyms of *strong*. |
| **free** | Look up antonyms of *catch*. |
| **friend** | A *friend* is someone you like and who likes you. There are many other words people can use instead of *friend* to show more exactly how good a *friend* someone is. |
| neighbor | A *neighbor* really means one who lives near you, but many people think of a *neighbor* as one who is friendly, willing to help you any time you need it, and who expects that you will do the same. |
| comrade | A *comrade* is a close friend. But the word did not always mean that. An ancient Latin word, "camera," meant a room where someone could stay overnight. In olden days travelers who stopped at an inn often had to share their rooms with several other people. A person who shared your room |

**friend** continued

became known as a "camarada." This word traveled into different languages and the meaning and spelling changed. Now *comrade* means a close friend. Soldiers in the army together are called *comrades*.

companion
chum
pal
buddy

A *companion* may be a close friend or one who goes with you. The two were *companions* on a trip. *Chum, pal,* and *buddy* are other words for a close friend.

ANTONYMS: enemy, foe

**Chum, pal,** and **buddy** are other words for a close friend.

**friendly**      Look up *kind*.
Look up antonyms of *cold*.

**friendship**      Look up *love* (n).

**frighten**      Look up *scare*.

**frightened**      Look up *afraid*.

**frightening**      Look up *scary*.

**frosty**      Look up *cold*.

# F

**full**

*Full* means having or holding as much as possible. It is the opposite of empty. A *full* glass of milk has no room for any more to be poured in. A *full* day has every minute taken up with something to be done. A *full* bus has no vacant seats and no place for another rider to stand.

heaping
overflowing

*Heaping* and *overflowing* mean more than full. A cup so full of sugar that the sugar is piled higher than the cup's edge is a *heaping* cupful. When a recipe calls for a *heaping* teaspoonful of cocoa, it means you must use more than just a teaspoon filled to the top with cocoa. If a cup is filled with water or other liquid that spills over the sides, it is an *overflowing* cup. An *overflowing* river is so full that water is pouring over its banks.

A **full** bus has no place for another rider.

loaded

*Loaded* means filled or covered with something. A *loaded* ship is one that has been filled with whatever cargo it is to carry, and has no room for anything more. A *loaded* gun has bullets in it. Our apple tree seemed *loaded* with blossoms this spring.

The apple tree seemed **loaded** with blossoms this spring.

stuffed

*Stuffed* means filled by being packed tightly. After a big dinner you may feel *stuffed*. *Stuffed* animals are cloth toys that are filled with soft materials. The opposite of *stuffed* is hollow.

crowded
jammed
crammed

*Crowded*, *jammed*, and *crammed* mean uncomfortably full. A *crowded* room may have too many people in it, or it may be filled with too much furniture. When an elevator has so many people in it that they can hardly move, it is *jammed*. This closet is so *crammed* that we can't get another thing in it.

ANTONYMS: empty, vacant, hollow, unloaded

**91**

**F**

| | |
|---|---|
| **funny** | *Funny* describes something that causes laughter. |
| amusing entertaining | An *amusing* story catches your attention in a pleasant way, makes you listen, and usually makes you laugh. An *entertaining* story holds your attention too. It is not boring or dull. But it does not always make you laugh. It may be sad and may make you cry. |
| humorous | *Humorous* describes anything that makes you laugh. A *humorous* story or happening may delight you because it is funny. People can make you laugh too. A *humorous* person sees the funny side of things, enjoys it, and points it out to others in a kindly way. |
| witty | *Witty* people are quick to see something funny or strange and to surprise you with it. They may not always be funny. *Witty* people may even be unkind. A *witty* remark may make you laugh, but it may hurt someone's feelings. |
| comical | *Comical* means funny enough to make you laugh a great deal. It was *comical* to see a clown riding backwards on a horse. Leroy told us a *comical* story about your trip. |

It was **comical** to see a clown riding backwards on a horse.

Something **hilarious** makes everyone roar with laughter.

| | |
|---|---|
| hilarious | Something *hilarious* makes you roar with laughter. It is more than just funny. We had a *hilarious* time at the party. |
| laughable | Anything *laughable* makes you laugh whether it is meant to be funny or not. The story Amy told to explain her mistake was *laughable*. The idea of our team beating the champions was *laughable*. |
| ridiculous | A *ridiculous* happening makes you laugh, but you often feel pity rather than pleasure from it. Johnny looked so *ridiculous* with pie all over his face that we had to laugh.<br><br>Look up *queer* for other words you might decide to use instead.<br><br>ANTONYMS: boring, dull, sad |
| **furious** | Look up *mad*. |

# G

**gallant**     Look up *brave*.

**gallop**     Look up *run*.

**gay**     Look up *happy* and *bright*.
Look up antonyms of *dim*.

**gaze**     Look up *look*.

**gentle**     Look up *soft* and *kind*.
Look up antonyms of *hard* and *rough*.

**get**     *Get* is the opposite of give. *Get* means come to own or to have something. You can *get* a letter or *get* a present or *get* a dish from the shelf. It can also mean become. You *get* older or *get* cold or *get* sick. I *got* what I wanted for my birthday. It *had gotten* quite cold during the night. I *have got* two dimes.

The words *got* and *gotten* are used all the time by almost everyone. But there are other ways of saying what you mean. You might say "It had become quite cold during the night," or "I have two dimes."

receive     *Receive* is the opposite of give or send. It means get something that has been given or sent or handed to you. You *receive* mail or information. You could even *receive* a black eye if someone gave you one.

obtain     To *obtain* something you must try in some way to get it. You may *obtain* a hat by buying it or *obtain* a book you want by borrowing it from the library.

fetch     *Fetch* means go and get something and bring or take it somewhere. Please *fetch* me a glass of water.

Chuck **got** what he wanted for his birthday.

94

earn    *Earn* means do some kind of work for what you get or expect to get. Stacy baby-sat to *earn* money.

win    *Win* means get something when there is a contest. You *win* a race if you are faster than everyone who is racing against you. But you can lose the race if only one person is faster than you are. You *won* first prize if you had the lucky number. A champion boxer *wins* the title but may have to give it up, or relinquish it, later to someone who is better.

Rosita will **win** the race if she is faster than everyone who is racing against her.

buy    *Buy* is get something by paying for it. Father has stopped to *buy* food at the supermarket. Dora *bought* a book today. I *have bought* several magazines on fishing.

catch    *Catch* is often used to mean get a disease. I hope you won't *catch* my cold. I *caught* it from my cousin.

ANTONYMS: give, send, lose, give up, relinquish

The hunter saw one **giant** footprint in the snow.

An ice skater seems to **glide** over the ice.

| | |
|---|---|
| **giant** | Look up *large*. |
| **gigantic** | Look up *large*. |
| **giggle** | Look up *laugh*. |
| **give** | Look up antonyms of *get*. |
| **give up** | Look up antonyms of *get*. |
| **glad** | Look up *happy*.<br>Look up antonyms of *sad*. |
| **glance** | Look up *look*. |
| **glare** | Look up *look*. |
| **glaring** | Look up *bright*. |
| **gleaming** | Look up *bright*.<br>Look up antonyms of *dim*. |
| **glide** | Look up *fly*. |
| **glistening** | Look up *bright*. |
| **glittering** | Look up *bright*. |
| **gloomy** | Look up *dim*.<br>Look up antonyms of *bright*. |
| **glowing** | Look up *bright*.<br>Look up antonyms of *dim*. |
| **gnaw** | Look up *eat*. |

**go**

Amy **has left** her boots at home.

**leave**

**depart**

**progress**

**proceed**

**run**

*Go* is the opposite of stop and of come. It means start to move or move away from. When you *go* outside or *go* away or *go* swimming, you move from where you are or from doing what you are doing. Spring comes and *goes*. Traffic stops and *goes*. You *go* when the traffic light is green. They *went* as soon as they could. They *had gone* before we arrived.

*Leave* usually means go away from some place or from someone or without something. A train *leaves* this station every hour. Carlos *left* his friends and went on alone. *Leave* also means go away without something. Amy *has left* her boots at home.

*Depart* also means go away. This bus *departs* at noon, and another arrives two hours later. The boys *departed* without saying good-by.

*Progress* can mean go forward. We *progressed* very slowly because the traffic was heavy.

*Proceed* means go along a certain way or by a certain plan. We *proceeded* slowly because the sidewalks were covered with snow. They *proceeded* to the corner as they were told to do.

*Run* sometimes means go or work, when you are talking about motors or engines. My watch stopped yesterday, but it is *running* now. We can't make the record player *run*. Maybe we *ran* it too long this morning.

**go** continued on page 98 ▶

# G

retreat

*Retreat* means go back. My cat began to *retreat* when the dog appeared.

escape

*Escape* means go away or get away from something. Gas was *escaping* from the pipe. The robbers *escaped* from jail.

\* \* \*

Many words that are not really synonyms for *go* can be used to make our language sharper and more precise. Here are some other good words you might want to use instead.

disappear
vanish

*Disappear* and *vanish* mean go out of sight, or just cease to exist. Stay, remain, and appear are antonyms of these words. A plane *disappears* when it goes out of sight in the sky. Smoke *disappears* in the air. The fog *disappeared* when the sun came up. A magician makes objects seem to *disappear*. *Vanish* often is used when something *disappears* suddenly. I saw a face appear at the window, but it *vanished* instantly. Darkness *vanishes* when you turn on a light.

fade
melt

*Fade* and *melt* mean disappear gradually or go out of sight or out of hearing slowly. Colors *fade* when they become dimmer and dimmer. A person or a building can *fade* into the fog. A sound can *fade* in the distance. The sound of the whistle *faded* as the train sped away. Snow *melts* and disappears in spring. An ice-cream bar will *melt* if you don't eat it fast.

John's ice-cream bar will **melt** if he doesn't eat it fast.

The boys **rambled** all over Aunt Mattie's farm.

take off
blast off
fly

*Take off*, *blast off*, and *fly* mean go off the ground. The next plane will *take off* in an hour. Two rockets *blast off* tomorrow. *Take off* and *fly* are sometimes used to mean leave and suddenly go fast. The dog *took off* after the rabbit. I can stay for only a minute; then I must *fly*.

stray

*Stray* means go slowly and wander around without any particular goal—maybe even get lost. The cows *strayed* across the road and into a cornfield.

ramble

*Ramble* means wander about, in no particular hurry, with no particular goal. We *rambled* all over Aunt Mattie's farm, looking at whatever interested us.

travel
cruise

*Travel* means take a trip. We *traveled* to the Rockies on our vacation. *Cruise* means take a trip on a boat. But it also means travel slowly. The police car *cruised* down the street looking for the lost dog.

ANTONYMS: stop, come, arrive, stay, remain, appear

**goal**          Look up *end* (n).

**gobble**        Look up *eat*.

# G

**good**

*Good* is the opposite of bad. It is also a word that is used too often and used to describe too many things. Almost anything that pleases you when you see, hear, taste, smell, or touch it may be called *good.*

*Good* can describe anything that is helpful, right, or pleasant. A pencil with a *good* point is helpful when you are writing a long list. *Good* pupils try to do their homework right. A *good* day is pleasant. A careful writer or speaker tries to use other words to describe something so clearly that people will know at once what is meant.

**useful**

If something is *useful,* it is good because it is helpful. A hammer is a *useful* tool for a carpenter. A watch makes a *useful* gift. My cousin gave me some *useful* ideas for earning money.

**valuable**

If something is *valuable,* it is very useful or worth a lot. Good tools are *valuable.* Friends are *valuable* because you wouldn't want to lose them. Losing a dollar bill makes you unhappy, but it could teach you a *valuable* lesson about taking care of your money.

**pleasant**

*Pleasant* describes something that gives you a good feeling. It is *pleasant* to listen to music that you like a lot. Going to an amusement park can be a *pleasant* way to spend the day. A cool breeze or a glass of ice water or a swim can all be *pleasant* on a hot day.

A cool breeze can be **pleasant** on a hot day.

excellent

*Excellent* means very, very good. It describes something that is useful or someone who is able to do something very well. Carl has some *excellent* ideas for our party. A lifeguard must be an *excellent* swimmer.

A **skilled** mechanic has repaired many cars.

skilled

*Skilled* means able to do something extremely well through much practice. A *skilled* carpenter has built many houses. A *skilled* mechanic has repaired many cars. An *excellent* baseball player may or may not be a *skilled* football player.

right

*Right* means good when it describes things that are not wrong or bad. The *right* answer to a question is a good one. The *right* place to cross a street is at the corner.

For other words you may want to use instead of *good*, look up *beautiful, brave, clean, funny, great, happy, interesting, kind, right, smart* (adj), *wonderful*. Also look up antonyms of *careless, dangerous, dim, dirty, mad, sad, stupid*.

The **right** place to cross the street is at the corner.

# G

| | |
|---|---|
| **gossip** | Look up *talk*. |
| **grab** | Look up *catch*. |
| **gradual** | Look up antonyms of *fast* (adj). |
| **gradually** | Look up antonyms of *fast* (adv). |
| **grand** | Look up *great*. |
| **graze** | Look up *eat*. |

In summer, flocks of sheep **graze** on the hillside.

**great** — *Great* can mean large. Then it is the opposite of little or small. *Great* also can mean important or excellent. Then it is the opposite of petty and trivial. A *great* man or a *great* woman may have done some outstanding deed or may have served his or her country well. Amelia Earhart was a *great* aviator. Albert Einstein was a *great* scientist. *Great* baseball players are listed in the Baseball Hall of Fame.

grand
magnificent — *Grand* and *magnificent* mean not only large but also dignified and inspiring. The band members in their new uniforms made a *grand* sight. Mrs. Garcia did a *magnificent* job of running the city when she was mayor.

**102**

A **stately** procession moved slowly down the aisle.

majestic
stately

*Majestic* and *stately* mean not only great in size but also great in appearance and dignity. The redwood tree looked *majestic* against the sky. A *stately* procession moved slowly down the aisle.

mighty

*Mighty* means large and strong or powerful. A *mighty* river thunders down the mountainside. A *mighty* roar came from the crowd.

tremendous

If something is *tremendous,* it is so large and powerful that it causes alarm or wonder or terror. A *tremendous* earthquake shook the buildings. The *tremendous* elephant pulled the truck out of the mud.

noble

*Noble* is great in appearance and action. A *noble* person is the opposite of a mean or petty person. The stranger had a *noble* face. Saving a life is a *noble* deed.

Look up *large* and *important* for other words you might want to use.

ANTONYMS: little, small, petty, trivial, mean

A watchdog **guards** a house.

| | |
|---|---|
| **grimy** | Look up *dirty*. |
| | Look up antonyms of *clean*. |
| **grin** | Look up *laugh*. |
| **grouchy** | Look up *mad*. |
| **guard** | Look up *keep*. |
| **guess** | Look up *think*. |
| **guffaw** | Look up *laugh*. |
| **guide** | Look up *show*. |
| **gulp** | Look up *eat*. |

**gyp**    *Gyp* is a word often used to mean keep or take something from someone dishonestly. A clerk in a store may *gyp* you if he doesn't give you enough change (though he might be making an honest mistake). You may feel that you have been *gypped* if you trade an arrowhead for a knife and then find that the knife blade is broken. A big boy *gypped* me out of first place in line by sneaking in ahead of me. The bubble-gum machine *gypped* me out of a penny.

The bubble-gum machine **gypped** Eduardo out of a penny.

cheat | *Cheat* means gyp, usually by doing something no one else notices. You *cheated* at checkers by moving your king when I wasn't looking.

mislead | *Mislead* means send in the wrong direction or away from the truth. If a street sign has been turned around, it may *mislead* you. Don't be *misled* by some TV advertisers.

trick | *Trick* means cheat someone by misleading or fooling that person. They *tricked* us into helping them clean up by promising us some chocolate cake. They knew all the time that there was no cake left.

deceive bamboozle | *Deceive* and *bamboozle* mean give a false impression in order to fool someone. The magician *deceived* us by making us think the hat was empty. I was completely *bamboozled* by Gwen's friendly smile. Then she hit me.

swindle | *Swindle* means cheat and take money by deceiving someone. I was *swindled*. I paid a dollar for this kite, and it's not worth a dime.

Joyce was **swindled.** She paid a dollar for the kite and it wasn't worth a dime.

bilk | *Bilk* means not pay someone what is owed. Some newspaper carriers know what *bilk* means. When they discover that one of their customers has moved away without paying this month's bill, they've been *bilked*.

# H

| | |
|---|---|
| **halt** | Look up *stop*. |
| **handsome** | Look up *beautiful*. |
| **happy** | *Happy* is the opposite of sad. *Happy* means feeling well and being contented and pleased with everybody and everything. You may be *happy* when you play with a friend. Or something can be called *happy* if it makes you feel good. You can have a *happy* vacation or hear the *happy* song of a bird. There are many other excellent words you can use to mean *happy*. |
| cheerful | *Cheerful* means full of good feeling and expecting the best. A person who is usually happy has a *cheerful* disposition. A *cheerful* person is not unhappy or always expecting the very worst to happen. |
| lighthearted | *Lighthearted* is happy with nothing to worry about. Hearing from the coach that you passed a swimming test can make you feel *lighthearted*. |
| glad | *Glad* usually means happy because of something good that has happened or will happen. Terry was *glad* she went to the party. Pablo will be *glad* to get your letter. |
| delighted | *Delighted* is stronger than glad. Grandmother was *delighted* with her present. The *delighted* boy thanked everyone for coming to his recital. |
| jubilant | *Jubilant* means showing great delight. It is a strong word for happy. Everyone in school was *jubilant* when we won the championship. |

Hearing that he had passed a swimming test made Robert feel **lighthearted**.

joyful
jolly
gay
merry

*Joyful, jolly, gay,* and *merry,* all mean feeling very, very happy and excited, perhaps laughing and joking. These feelings may not last very long—a person who is not always happy may feel *jolly* or *gay* or *merry* at a party. A party can be *jolly, gay,* or *merry* too.

A party can be **jolly, gay,** or **merry.**

contented
satisfied

*Contented* and *satisfied* mean happy with where you are or what you are doing or with the way things are going. The hamster seemed *contented* in its cage. Our teacher was *satisfied* with our work. This store has many *satisfied* customers.

ANTONYMS: sad, unhappy, downcast, mournful, sorrowful, miserable, wretched, woebegone

## hard

Cleaning a messy room is a **hard** job.

*Hard* is the opposite of easy when you speak of something that takes a lot of work or effort. It is *hard* to get out of bed on a cold morning. Cleaning your room is a *hard* job. Some directions are *hard* to follow.

*Hard* is the opposite of soft when you say a wooden bench is *hard*. You probably use *hard* to describe candy you can't bite or ice you can skate on or paste that has dried in the jar and won't spread.

*Hard* is the opposite of gentle when you say that a *hard* wind was blowing or that the villain in the story was a *hard* man.

### difficult

*Difficult* means not easy. You might use *difficult* when you talk of a problem or task that makes you think or come to some decision. You may have a *difficult* time deciding what to buy for a birthday present. A good book report can be *difficult* to write. Some books are *difficult* to read, even for a good reader.

### complicated

Something is *complicated* if it is difficult to understand or if it has so many parts that it is hard to take apart and put together. Car engines are *complicated*. Some very *complicated* puzzles are fun to work. A *complicated* explanation often is so long that you may be more confused than helped by it.

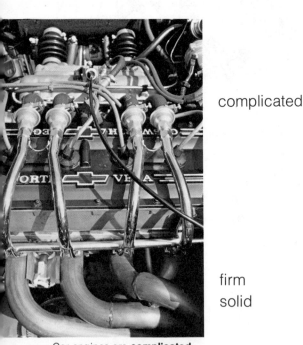

Car engines are **complicated**.

### firm
### solid

*Firm* and *solid* mean hard as the opposite of soft. They mean not easily moved out of place or out of shape. Ice on a pond is *firm* when it is so hard that it does not break or

A board is **rigid.**

sink when you walk on it. It is *solid* if it is frozen from top to bottom. A *solid* board has no holes or cracks in it.

**stiff**
**rigid**

*Stiff* and *rigid* mean unbending. They are the opposite of soft and limp. *Stiff* bristles in a brush are not easily bent. Your legs may feel *stiff* after you have sat in one position for a long time. It is hard to walk because your legs don't move easily. Something *rigid* is so *stiff* that it can't be bent without being broken. The doctor put my broken arm in a *rigid* cast. A board is *rigid*.

**tough**

*Tough* means firm and strong but not rigid and unbending. A piece of *tough* meat is firm and hard to chew. Tender meat is easy to chew. We may even call a difficult problem *tough*. A *tough* athlete has great endurance.

**severe**
**stern**
**harsh**

*Severe, stern,* and *harsh* mean hard as the opposite of soft or gentle or light. You may consider a person *severe* or *stern* who demands that a thing be done exactly right and does not allow any excuses or reasons for doing it another way. A *severe* or *harsh* punishment can hurt more than a light one. When your coach looks *severe* or *stern*, you probably don't argue with him. *Severe* and *harsh* can describe something not gentle or mild. A *severe* winter or a *harsh* wind is unpleasant and causes discomfort.

ANTONYMS: easy, soft, gentle, limp (adj), tender, light, mild, simple

# H

A **hardy** plant can live through very cold weather.

| | |
|---|---|
| **hardy** | Look up *strong*. |
| **harm** | Look up *hurt*. |
| **harmful** | Look up *bad*. |
| **harmless** | Look up antonyms of *dangerous*. |
| **harsh** | Look up *rough* and *hard*. |
| | Look up antonyms of *soft*. |
| **hasten** | Look up *hurry*. |
| **hastily** | Look up *fast* (adv). |
| **hasty** | Look up *fast* (adj). |

The children **hastened** to tell their teacher what had happened.

**hate**

People often use *hate* when they don't really mean it. Sometimes they use it to mean merely the opposite of like. You may say you *hate* carrots or *hate* to go to bed early, when you really mean you're not fond of carrots or you prefer not to go to bed early. You may say you *hate* your best friend, but you really mean you're a bit angry at him or her right at this moment.

*Hate* is a very strong word. It is the opposite of love. If you really *hate* something, you have such a strong feeling that you may want to break it or hurt it as much as you can.

Ned may say he **hates** carrots but he really means he's not fond of them.

dislike

*Dislike* means not enjoy or not approve of something or someone. I *dislike* Western movies, but I enjoy stories about the Old West. Cats *dislike* getting wet.

despise

*Despise* is stronger than dislike. You *despise* something if you dislike it so much that you think it is not worth noticing. You probably *despise* name-calling.

detest

If you dislike something very much, you *detest* it. You may *detest* doing the dishes but enjoy running the vacuum cleaner. You may like to paint but *detest* cleaning up.

loathe

If you shudder at the thought of touching or getting near something, you *loathe* it. Some people *loathe* crawly things. Wilbur *loathed* spiders, especially hairy ones.

ANTONYMS: like, be fond of, love (v), enjoy

# H

Some trucks **haul** huge logs.

**haul**       Look up *pull*.

**hazardous**  Look up *dangerous*.

**heal**       Look up antonyms of *break*.

**heaping**    Look up *full*.

**heavy**      Look up antonyms of *thin*.

**help**       *Help* means supply whatever someone needs or do whatever must be done for him or her. You *help* a friend with a garden or *help* someone carry packages. Some medicine *helps* when you are sick. Persons in great danger cry "*Help!*" when they cannot do anything to *help* themselves. Something that is meant to *help* you may hinder you instead.

aid        *Aid* means help, but it is not quite so strong a word. You may *aid* people by working along with them. Pupils can *aid* in a drive to collect clothes or money. Money will *aid* in building a new hospital. Lack of

**help** continued

money can obstruct or hinder it. The Red Cross does everything it can to *aid* people who are caught in a flood.

Carmen **supported** the sick man until they found a chair.

cooperate
: Two people or nations *cooperate* when they work together on a project or a job that will help them both. States *cooperate* in building highways. One citizen not only refused to *cooperate* with the committee but promised to oppose everything it did.

support
: You *support* someone if you help him walk or sit up by letting his weight rest on you. Carmen *supported* the sick man until they found a chair. *Support* also means help by supplying all the money one needs. Mothers and fathers usually *support* their families.

assist
: *Assist* means help someone do something by working with him or her. You *assist* an old person across the street or up the stairs. A librarian may *assist* you in finding the book you want. A nurse may *assist* by handing instruments to a doctor.

improve
: *Improve* means help by making something better. Painting the house *improved* its appearance. Salt *improves* the taste of some vegetables. Winning this game will *improve* our chances of getting the trophy.

encourage
: *Encourage* is help by giving hope to someone. You *encouraged* me when you said I played well enough to get into the band.

ANTONYMS: hinder, obstruct, oppose

# H

**helpful**   Look up *kind*.

**heroic**   Look up *brave*.

**hide**   *Hide* means put or be out of sight. You can *hide* a pencil or *hide* your face behind your hands. You *hid* yourself when you played hide-and-seek. A thing may be *hidden* on purpose or by accident. Birthday presents can be *hidden* until the day of a surprise party. In a snapshot one person's head may *hide* another person's face.

In a snapshot one person's head may **hide** another person's face.

cover   *Cover* can mean hide by putting something over and around. They *covered* their footprints with leaves. Snow *covered* the path. We *covered* the cracks in the wall with pictures.

bury   *Bury* means hide by covering with a large amount of something. Pirates *buried* treasure in the ground. Cars might get *buried* in a snowdrift during a snowstorm. The magazine you want has been *buried* under a whole pile of papers.

conceal

*Conceal* usually means hide or cover up something on purpose so that it won't be discovered. Birds that build their nests on the ground *conceal* them in the grass. Bob tried to *conceal* the kitten under his jacket. The kitten revealed itself by poking its head out. I wanted to *conceal* the plans for an anniversary party from my parents, but my little sister disclosed them.

disguise

*Disguise* means change the look of something or someone so it won't be recognized. A young actor disguises herself to play the part of an old woman. Some people *disguise* their true feelings by acting just the opposite of the way they feel.

mask

*Mask* means hide by making something hard to recognize or see. The poet *masked* his real meaning by using words that mean something else.

ANTONYMS: reveal, disclose, discover, unmask, find, show

**hideous**  Look up antonyms of *beautiful*.

**hike**  Look up *walk*.

**hilarious**  Look up *funny*.

**hinder**  Look up antonyms of *help*.

**hit-or-miss**  Look up *careless*.

**hobble**  Look up *walk*.

**hold**  Look up *keep*.

**hollow**  Look up *empty*.
Look up antonyms of *full*.

A young actor **disguises** herself to play the part of an old woman.

115

Some birds **hop** around on the ground looking for worms.

| | |
|---|---|
| **homely** | Look up antonyms of *beautiful*. |
| **hop** | Look up *jump*. |
| **horrible** | Look up *awful*. |
| **horrid** | Look up antonyms of *beautiful*. |
| **horrifying** | Look up *scary*. |

**hot**      *Hot* describes something that feels warmer than things around it or warmer than your body. *Hot* also describes something that gives you a burning feeling when you touch, taste, or get near it. A stove can be *hot*, but so can pepper. *Hot* can also mean angry, as in a *hot* temper.

*Hot* is used in many ways—a *hot* day, a *hot* news story, a *hot* chase. There are many other words that can be used instead of *hot* even though they are not all synonyms.

A **warm** coat feels good.

burning      *Burning* describes something hot enough to be painful—the *burning* sand on the desert.

steaming      *Steaming* is hot enough to turn water into mist. A tub of *steaming* water or a cup of *steaming* cocoa is very hot. A *steaming* jungle would feel hot and wet and sticky.

warm      *Warm* means just hot enough to be comfortable or to give comfort. A *warm* coat feels good. A spring wind is *warm*. Cool is the opposite of *warm*.

tepid      Something neither hot nor cold may be called *tepid*. Hot food may cool until it is *tepid* and not very pleasant to eat.

fiery

*Fiery* means full of fire or flaming. Steel in a blast furnace is *fiery*. The traveler in the desert could not stand the *fiery* sun any longer. Icy winds are sometimes as unbearable as a *fiery* sun. You may say someone who becomes angry very easily has a *fiery* temper. A swallow of food that is loaded with pepper would be *fiery* in your throat.

flushed

*Flushed* means hot and red, usually in the face. Your face may be *flushed* if you have a fever, if you are angry, or if you have just done a lot of running and exercising.

sultry

Air is *sultry* when it is hot and damp and sticky before a thunderstorm.

torrid

*Torrid* means unbearably hot and dry. The sun is usually *torrid* over the desert.

sweltering

*Sweltering* means hot enough to make you feel limp and tired. On a *sweltering* day you just want to sit in the shade of a tree.

sizzling

*Sizzling* means hot enough to burn or cook with a hissing sound. A frying pan full of *sizzling* bacon sounds and smells good.

peppery

*Peppery* food is stinging to the taste because it is seasoned with lots of pepper or other spices.

ANTONYMS: cool, cold, icy, mild

The sun is usually **torrid** over the desert.

# H

**hover**       Look up *fly*.

**howl**       Look up *laugh* and *say*.

**hubbub**       Look up *noise*.

**huge**       Look up *large*.
               Look up antonyms of *little*.

**humorous**       Look up *funny*.

**hurdle**       Look up *jump*.

In this race the runners have to **hurdle** a bush and a stream.

**hurl**       Look up *throw*.

**hurry**       *Hurry* means move quickly or make someone or something move quickly. *Hurry* so you won't be late. Don't dawdle while you are dressing. We have to *hurry* Junior along or we'll surely miss the plane. Can you *hurry* your work a little?

She had to **rush** through breakfast in order to catch her train.

| | |
|---|---|
| rush<br>hasten | *Rush* and *hasten* mean move or push forward in a great hurry. Yesterday Mother had to *rush* through breakfast in order to catch her train. If she had lingered over her orange juice one minute longer, she would have missed it. The children *hastened* to tell their teacher what had happened. |
| speed | To *speed* sometimes means to go very fast. When cars *speed*, they often are slowed down by police officers. The fire trucks *sped* to the blaze. |
| hustle | *Hustle* means push onward quickly. After breakfast Grandpa *hustled* us off to school. He told us not to loiter on the way. |
| dash | *Dash* also means move swiftly, but for only a short distance. Todd had to *dash* to catch the ball before it hit the ground. I *dashed* to the corner to catch the bus. |
| fly | *Fly* is a good word for hurry. We'll never make it to the parade if we don't *fly* the minute school is over. |

ANTONYMS: dawdle, linger, slow down, loiter

# H

**hurt**

*Hurt* has several meanings. It can mean cause pain to the body or to someone's feelings. You can *hurt* yourself if you fall off a horse. She *has hurt* my feelings by making fun of my new sweater. *Hurt* also means feel pain. My wrist *hurts* when I try to pick anything up.

*Hurt* can also mean damage something. I hope the rain won't *hurt* my new shoes. Losing the game *has hurt* our chances of winning the championship this year.

harm

*Harm* means give or cause pain. Telling a lie could *harm* other people. Nothing can *harm* you here.

Lilly said, "Nothing can **harm** you here."

damage

*Damage* means hurt or lower the value of something. Reading for a long time in a dim light can *damage* your eyes. The holes in the road *damaged* the front tire on the truck.

The tumble he took down the stairs made Martin's arm **ache**.

injure     *Injure* means wound or hurt someone. You might *injure* yourself and others if you're not careful where you ride your bike.

mar     *Mar* means hurt by changing or spoiling the appearance of something. Smudges will *mar* a newly washed window. A deep scratch *marred* the tabletop. Our new sidewalk was *marred* by footprints during the night.

spoil     *Spoil* means hurt beyond repair. I *spoiled* my soap carving by cutting too deep. Too much pepper *spoiled* the soup.

ache     *Ache* means suffer or feel pain. The tumble I took down the stairs made my arm *ache*.

sting
smart     *Sting* and *smart* mean suffer sharp, quick pain. If you catch a hard ball with your bare hand, your hand will *sting*. My eyes *stung* from the smoke. They *have stung* all day. Medicine put on a cut finger sometimes makes it *smart* or *sting*.

**hustle**     Look up *hurry*.

# I

**icy**       Look up *cold*.
Look up antonyms of *hot*.

**imagine**       Look up *think*.

**immense**       Look up *large*.

**impatient**       Look up *excited*.

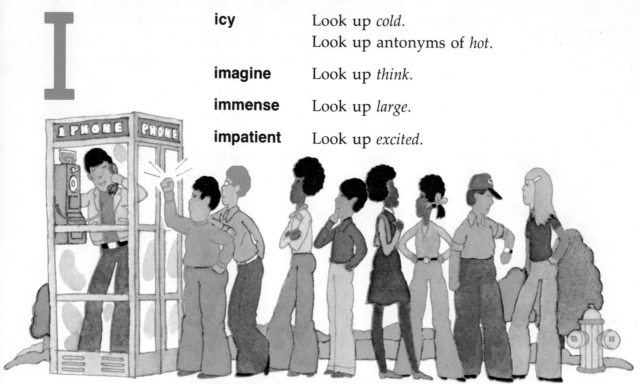

Some people are very **impatient** if they have to wait in line.

**important**       *Important* means very useful or having great worth or value. It is the opposite of trivial. A steering wheel is an *important* part of an automobile. A meeting of two leaders could be *important* to their people. The President makes *important* decisions as well as minor ones every day. *Important* also means great or large. A city or river may be *important*.

famous       *Famous* means well known and usually well liked or respected. People often become *famous* for something important they have done or for some important job they hold. Chief Joseph was a *famous* leader of the Nez Percé Indians. "Liberty and justice for all" are *famous* words.

**122**

Rungs are **essential** to a ladder.

**important** continued

essential
necessary

Something that is *essential* or *necessary* is so important that a person or object could not get along without it. Food is *essential* to people and animals. Rungs are *essential* to a ladder. I couldn't put together this model plane because an *essential* piece was missing. Good brakes are *necessary* on a car. Learning how to study is a *necessary* part of school.

valuable

*Valuable* means important because of being very useful or worth a lot of money. Lisa learned a *valuable* lesson when she had to copy her whole paragraph over because no one could read it. Practice time is *valuable* to a musician or an athlete. A big athlete is *valuable* to a football team. *Valuable* papers and jewels should be kept in a safe place.

Look up *great* and *large* for other words you might want to use.

ANTONYMS: minor, trivial, unimportant

**imprison**       Look up *shut.*

**improper**       Look up antonyms of *right.*

**improve**        Look up *help.*

**impure**         Look up *dirty.*
                   Look up antonyms of *clean.*

**inappropriate**  Look up antonyms of *right.*

**incorrect**      Look up antonyms of *right.*

**indifferent**    Look up antonyms of *excited.*

**injure**         Look up *hurt.*

**inquire**        Look up *ask.*

# I

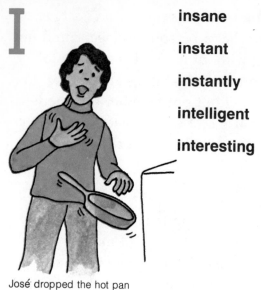

José dropped the hot pan **instantly**.

**insane**    Look up *mad*.

**instant**    Look up *fast* (adj).

**instantly**    Look up *fast* (adv).

**intelligent**    Look up *smart* (adj).

**interesting**    *Interesting* means holding your attention. Whatever holds your attention is not boring or dull. You can read an *interesting* book, hear an *interesting* story, take an *interesting* trip, or meet an *interesting* person. But many other words can be used to describe more precisely how *interesting* something is.

entertaining    *Entertaining* describes someone or something that holds your attention in a pleasant and enjoyable way. Someone who performs tricks or tells funny stories can be *entertaining*. Feeding time at the zoo is an *entertaining* sight.

amusing    *Amusing* means even more enjoyable than entertaining. An *amusing* book makes you laugh. You enjoy it so much you feel good even after you finish it. It is an *amusing* sight to see my kitten playing with a string. Our teacher read the class a very *amusing* poem.

fascinating    *Fascinating* means so interesting that it pulls your attention like a magnet. The detective's solution of the mystery made a *fascinating* story. The magician did some *fascinating* tricks with a quarter and a dime.

The TV show was so **absorbing** that Kimiko didn't hear anyone call her to supper.

| | |
|---|---|
| absorbing | The word *absorb* means soak up like a sponge, so *absorbing* means soaking up your attention. A TV show may be so *absorbing* that you don't hear anyone call you to supper. |
| exciting<br>thrilling | *Exciting* and *thrilling* mean interesting enough to make you feel happy or afraid or shivery. An *exciting* race will hold your attention. Riding on a roller coaster is *exciting*. A *thrilling* rescue or a *thrilling* end to a movie may give you goose pimples. A band playing "The Star-Spangled Banner" can be *thrilling* to hear. |

ANTONYMS: boring, dull, uninteresting

| | |
|---|---|
| **introduce** | Look up *start*.<br>Look up antonyms of *end* (v). |
| **invent** | Look up *make* and *start*. |
| **irritable** | Look up *mad*. |
| **irritated** | Look up *mad*. |
| **isolated** | Look up *lonely*. |

**125**

# J

| | |
|---|---|
| **jammed** | Look up *full*. |
| **jaunt** | Look up *trip* (n). |
| **jog** | Look up *run*. |
| **jolly** | Look up *happy*. |
| **journey** | Look up *trip* (n). |
| **joyful** | Look up *happy*. |
| **jubilant** | Look up *happy*. |

**jump**

*Jump* means throw yourself into the air. It also means to leave the ground or a surface as if thrown into the air. The cat *jumped* onto the table, but we made it *jump* off at once. The fans *jumped* up and down as they watched the football game.

But *jump* is often used differently too. A train *jumps* the track if it goes off the rails. You say you *jump* when a sudden noise makes your body jerk—but you don't really leave the ground. You can win at checkers by *jumping* your opponent's kings. But you really move your king over her king. To start a race the starter shoots a gun. Anyone who starts to run before the shot is fired *jumps the gun*. So if you begin something too soon, you *jump the gun*.

Rochelle said, "If you start too soon, you **jump the gun**."

spring
leap

*Spring* and *leap* mean jump. A cowboy may *spring* into the saddle. The basketball players *sprang* to their feet. The dog *had sprung* through the door as it opened. Elena can *leap* across a stream.

| | |
|---|---|
| bound<br>skip | *Bound* and *skip* mean move quickly with many leaps. The deer *bounded* into the woods. Pat *skipped* down the sidewalk. Many athletes *skip* rope. |

| | |
|---|---|
| hop | *Hop* means jump on one foot or jump with both feet together. If you drop a rock on one foot, you might *hop* around on the other foot. Some birds *hop* around on the ground looking for worms. |
| vault | *Vault* means jump or leap over something by using your hands or a pole. You can *vault* a fence by putting your hands on it and swinging yourself over. |

Matt can **vault** a fence by putting his hands on it and swinging himself over.

| | |
|---|---|
| hurdle | *Hurdle* means jump over something while running. In this race we have to *hurdle* a bush and a stream. |
| dive<br>plunge | *Dive* and *plunge* mean jump or be thrown suddenly downward or into something, usually headfirst. You *dive* from a diving board into the pool. The coach *dived* (or *dove*) twice to show me how to do it. You might run down the beach and *plunge* into the water. |

Just as *jump* is used for other actions, some of its synonyms are used when you don't really mean *jump*. For example, if you miss a line in a book you are reading, you have *skipped* the line. A person sometimes *hurdles* a problem if he or she faces it and overcomes or solves it. You may *plunge* into a hard job and get it done.

| | |
|---|---|
| **just** | Look up *right*. |

127

# K

Karen **keeps** goldfish.

**keep**

*Keep* means hold on to. It's smart to *keep* part of your allowance. Some people *keep* shoes that are worn out. Other people discard them.

*Keep* also means take care of. You may *keep* goldfish or *keep* your neighbors' lawn or *keep* their dog when they go away. *Keep* can also mean stay off or away from, or it can mean make someone or something stay off or away from. You *kept* off the grass in summer and *kept* the snow off the sidewalk in winter. Rain *has kept* you inside. You *keep* from talking if you *keep* still.

save
preserve
conserve

*Save, preserve,* and *conserve* are other words for keep. Most people try to *save* money or *save* time. The government tries to *preserve* parts of this country and keep them as they were in the days before the Pilgrims landed. Travelers in a desert must *conserve* their supply of water. Long-distance swimmers must *conserve* their strength.

hold

*Hold* can mean keep from. If you *hold* your tongue, you keep from speaking. When soldiers *held* their fire, they kept from shooting.

tend

*Tend* means take care of something. You *tend* flowers that you have planted. A storekeeper *tends* the store.

protect
guard

*Protect* and *guard* mean take care of and keep from harm or damage. An umbrella *protects* you from the rain. A watchdog *guards* a house.

ANTONYMS: discard, lose, let go, throw away

128

| | |
|---|---|
| **kind** | A *kind* person is one who is interested in others. He or she is never cruel. A *kind* deed is one that helps someone. Many other words describe someone who is *kind* or something that shows kindness. |
| helpful<br>thoughtful<br>considerate | A *helpful* person will do anything to help you. *Thoughtful* and *considerate* people are careful of the feelings of others. They think about what others want and need, rather than only what they themselves want. Remembering someone's birthday is a *thoughtful* thing to do. It is *considerate* to play a guest's favorite game when she or he comes to your house. |
| gentle | A *gentle* person is not rough or mean. |
| pleasant<br>friendly | *Pleasant* and *friendly* describe people who are fun to be with and who are interested in you. A *pleasant* person is not ugly or quarrelsome. |
| sympathetic | A *sympathetic* person listens to your troubles, understands your problems, and knows how you feel. |
| tactful | *Tactful* means careful of another's feelings. A *tactful* person tries to correct someone's mistake without making that person angry. |

Remembering someone's birthday is a **thoughtful** thing to do.

ANTONYMS: cruel, rough, mean, ugly, quarrelsome, unpleasant, unkind, cold

# L

**large**     *Large* is the opposite of little or small. *Large* means bigger in size or amount than other things like it—a *large* stone or a *large* bunch of grapes or a *large* city. The word *large* is used for many things of different sizes. People can't really tell what you mean when you call something *large* unless you are comparing its size to something else. If you see three pieces of pie and say "I'll take the *large* one," then people know what you mean by *large*.

huge     *Huge* can mean having or containing a large amount of something. An ocean is a *huge* body of water. I had a *huge* dish of ice cream. I saw a *huge* dog.

vast     *Vast* means stretching over a large area. A *vast* desert stretched ahead of us.

immense enormous     *Immense* and *enormous* describe something so large that the size can hardly be imagined. The sky seems *immense* when you lie on the ground and look up at it. An *enormous* yellow moon came up over the lake.

Debbie saw a **huge** dog.

giant
gigantic

*Giant* and *gigantic* also mean very much larger than other objects. The hunter saw one *giant* footprint in the snow. A *gigantic* tree towered above the others in the forest.

colossal

*Colossal* describes something tremendously large, usually something that has been built by people. This word has an interesting history.

Many, many years ago there was an ancient Greek city called Rhodes. The people of Rhodes had a gigantic statue of their sun god built near their harbor. Today no one knows for sure what the bronze statue looked like because it was destroyed by an earthquake. It was supposed to have been over one hundred feet tall and may have held a torch in one hand to lead ships into the harbor. Because the ancient Greek word for a gigantic statue was "kolossos," the statue was called the "Colossus of Rhodes."

We still call a gigantic statue a "colossus." We might refer to a huge person as a "colossus." A skyscraper or a bridge or anything really large we call *colossal*.

Look up *great* and *important* for other words you might want to use.

ANTONYMS: little, small, tiny, fine

Some people call a gigantic statue a "colossus."

# L

**laugh**

When you *laugh* you show joy or amusement by the look on your face and by making a certain sound. You can *laugh* at a joke or at an amusing sight. Many words describe different ways of laughing even though these words are not all synonyms.

smile
grin

*Smile* and *grin* are not the same as laugh, but you might consider them weak words for laugh. When you *smile,* your eyes brighten and the corners of your mouth turn up. When you *grin,* you smile but you open your lips and show your teeth. By *smiling* or *grinning* you are able to show amusement or joy without making any sound at all.

chuckle

You *chuckle* when you laugh very quietly. Babies *chuckle* sometimes when you play with them.

giggle

You *giggle* when you keep catching your breath and making a continuous noise as you laugh. People sound foolish if they *giggle* too much. Sometimes you *giggle* when you are nervous or embarrassed rather than when you are amused or happy.

When Concha **smiles,** the corners of her mouth turn up.

When Terry **grins,** he shows his teeth.

Dean **giggles** when he makes a continuous noise as he laughs.

When Yoko **guffaws,** she just opens her mouth and lets out a great big laugh.

| | |
|---|---|
| snicker | You *snicker* if you laugh but try to cover it up. Sometimes when something funny happens in class you can't help but *snicker*. |
| guffaw | When you *guffaw,* you just open your mouth and let out a great big laugh, usually about something that strikes you as very funny. This is a very strong word for laugh. |
| howl<br>roar | *Howl* and *roar* are ways in which animals make noise, but we sometimes say people *howl* or *roar* with laughter. |

**laughable**   Look up *funny*.

**launch**   Look up *start*.
Look up antonyms of *end* (v).

To **launch** a boat, someone puts it into the water for the first time.

**lay**   Look up *put*.

**lead**   Look up *show*.

**lean**   Look up *thin*.

**leap**   Look up *jump*.

# L

**leave**       Look up *go*.
Look up antonyms of *carry*, of *choose*, and of *come*.

**lenient**     Look up *soft*.

**let go**      Look up antonyms of *carry*, of *catch*, and of *keep*.

**level**       Look up *smooth*.

**light**       Look up *bright*.
Look up antonyms of *hard*.

**lighthearted**  Look up *happy*.

**like**        *Like* means feel agreeable toward or pleased with someone or something. You may *like* your teacher or *like* candy or *like* swimming. It also means have a wish for something. Maybe you'd *like* to be a teacher when you grow up.

enjoy
be fond of   *Enjoy* may be used if you speak of taking pleasure in something. *Be fond of* is used for something you like very much. You *enjoy* swimming or *enjoy* a good book. You probably wouldn't say you *are fond of* a good book, but you could *be fond of* candy. You may *enjoy* eating, but you *are fond of* food.

admire     You *admire* someone if you like what that person has done or the kind of person he or she is. You might *admire* a dancer or a courageous explorer. You might *admire* a beautiful object—but you can't always use *admire* for like. You may *admire* your teacher or his new jacket, but you wouldn't *admire* candy or swimming.

Leon **wants** to be famous.

| | |
|---|---|
| want | *Want* means desire very much or even need something. Many nations *want* freedom. Leon *wants* to be famous. |
| love | *Love* is stronger than like. You *love* something or someone. But many people use it even for things they care just a little for, so *love* is a worn-out word. It's a good idea to use other words that tell more exactly how you feel, and save *love* for things and people that really mean the most to you.

ANTONYMS: dislike, hate, loathe |

| | |
|---|---|
| **liking** | Look up *love* (n). |
| **limit** | Look up *end* (n). · |
| **limp** (adj) | Look up antonyms of *hard*. |
| **limp** (v) | Look up *walk*. |
| **linger** | Look up antonyms of *hurry*. |

# L

**little**

*Little* means less than other things in size or amount or value. It is the opposite of big or large. The *little* bear was not as big as the other two bears.

small
tiny

You can use *small* and *tiny* instead of little when you are talking about the size of someone or something. You might speak of a *small* child or a *tiny* child. You wouldn't use *small* or *tiny* if you were talking about the amount of something. A little candy usually means a few pieces of candy. A *small* or *tiny* candy would mean one piece that was very little. If you ask for a little milk, you mean a *small* amount.

fine

*Fine* can mean small. Print that is so small you can hardly read the words is called *fine* print. Something that is ground into very small pieces may be called *fine*— *fine* sugar or *fine* sand.

"I can hardly read this **fine** print," Cheryl said.

scanty
skimpy

*Scanty* and *skimpy* are not really synonyms of little, but they are good words to describe something that is too little or not quite enough. You had a *scanty* breakfast if you did not have nearly as much as you wanted. Dresses or slacks that fit but that have no extra material at the hem so they can be lengthened can be called *skimpy*. You write a *skimpy* book report if you don't tell enough for anyone else to know what the book is about.

ANTONYMS: big, large, bulky, great, huge

| | |
|---|---|
| **loaded** | Look up *full.* |
| **loathe** | Look up *hate.* |
| | Look up antonyms of *like.* |
| **locate** | Look up *find.* |
| **loiter** | Look up antonyms of *hurry.* |

The Whitefeathers must **locate** a gas station.

**lonely**

*Lonely* means being away from others. *Lonely* and all of its synonyms can describe how a person feels or how something looks. When *lonely* is used to describe people, it usually means feeling sad because of being away from friends or family. A *lonely* child sitting on a curb probably wishes for company. But when you speak of one *lonely* tree high on a hill, you don't mean the tree is feeling sad. You mean that it is the only tree there. A *lonely* road is not sad, but it is without houses or much traffic.

alone

*Alone* means being away from others or being the only one of its kind. It does not mean feeling sad. A person who lives *alone* may not feel lonely.

lonesome

*Lonesome* usually means sad because you are lonely. You may be *lonesome* for a friend.

forlorn

*Forlorn* is stronger than lonesome. If you are all alone in a crowd of strangers, you may feel *forlorn.* You are not away from others, but you feel lonely. The little boy looked *forlorn* as he waved good-by.

**lonely** continued on page 138 ▶

**137**

**lonely** continued from page 137

isolated

*Isolated* means cut off or set apart from others. A cabin that is all by itself in the mountains is *isolated*. A person with mumps is *isolated* from other people.

desolate

*Desolate* means very, very lonely and away from others. If you have lost a friend, you may be *desolate*. A farm many miles away from other farms may be a *desolate* place, even though people live there.

**lonesome**

Look up *lonely*.

The two boys **looked at** the sky and **saw** millions of stars.

**look**

*Look* or *look at* means take in or understand something by using the eyes. To *look*, you focus your eyes on something.

see

*See* and *look* mean almost the same thing. *See* means take in the sight of something. You *see* a movie. Maybe you *have seen* it before. Perhaps you *saw* it last week. You can *see* daylight without *looking at* it. We *looked at* the sky and *saw* millions of stars.

behold
: *Behold* is often used instead of look at when attention is being called to something. A magician may say, "*Behold*, an empty hat!" Then, as you are looking at it, pull a rabbit out. You *behold* a lofty mountain. The mountain climbers *beheld* a secret valley.

observe
: *Observe* means look at closely and carefully. A magician may say, "*Observe* the coin in my hand." Then, as you are looking at it, make it disappear. People *observe* birds by looking through field glasses.

view
: *View* can be used instead of look at. You *view* television. You wouldn't *observe* it or *behold* it. You *view* a sunset or a magnificent sight when you look at it.

glance
: You *glance* at something when you look at it for just a moment. I *glanced* in the window as I passed the store. Kay *glanced* at me, then turned away.

gaze
: You *gaze* when you look for a long time. You may *gaze* at a bee on a flower. You may *gaze* out the window, looking at nothing in particular.

stare
: If you *stare* at something, you look a long time at it, perhaps without blinking your eyes. We *stared* at the newspaper because we couldn't believe the headline. Many people think it is impolite to *stare*.

glare
: If someone *glares* at you, he or she looks at you angrily. The bus driver *glared* at us for shouting.

**look** continued on page 140 ▶

They **stared** at the newspaper because they couldn't believe the headline.

Opal **peered** at the sign because she had lost her glasses.

| | |
|---|---|
| peer | *Peer* means look closely and curiously. Opal *peered* at the sign because she had lost her glasses. I *peered* down into the hole. |
| peek | You *peek* at something secretly or from a hiding place. We *peeked* at the presents on the shelf. Dan *peeked* through a hole in the fence. |
| watch | *Watch* means look at or observe for a long time in order to follow the movement of something or in order to be ready for something. You may *watch* a ball game. You can *watch* the sun go down or *watch* the cat so that it doesn't claw the furniture. |
| examine | You *examine* something if you look it over very carefully and completely. The umpire *examined* the ball before throwing it back into the game. The dog *examined* the bone before beginning to chew on it. The doctor *examined* my throat. |

| loom | Look up *come*. |
| lope | Look up *run*. |
| lose | Look up antonyms of *get*, of *find*, and of *keep*. |

**loud**

*Loud* is the opposite of quiet and soft. *Loud* means having or making a big sound. You may hear a *loud* noise or speak in a *loud* voice or drop a book with a *loud* bang.

noisy

*Noisy* describes a lot of loud, harsh sounds. Boys and girls can have a *noisy* game of tag or a quiet game of checkers. A lot of traffic on a street is *noisy*.

shrill

*Shrill* means having or making a loud, high, sharp sound. The sound of a whistle is *shrill*. When some children play, their voices grow *shrill*. A soft voice is the opposite of a *shrill* or loud voice.

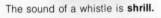

The sound of a whistle is **shrill.**

boisterous

*Boisterous* means loud and noisy. The *boisterous* children outside shouted. When they came inside, they spoke in subdued voices.

thunderous

*Thunderous* describes a loud noise that sounds like thunder. The cast received *thunderous* applause. A big waterfall sounds *thunderous*. It is never still.

roaring

A long, loud, deep sound is *roaring*. The *roaring* fire was hard to put out. *Roaring* planes flew low.

ANTONYMS: quiet (adj), soft, subdued, still, silent

**love** (n)   *Love* is a strong feeling of being drawn to a person or to an object. You may feel *love* for someone if you admire and enjoy being with that person and want to do anything you can to make that person happy.

*Love* of an object is a desire to have or enjoy it because it is beautiful or delightful, or because it seems that you must have it in order to be happy.

affection   *Affection* is a kind, warm feeling for someone or something. It is not as strong as love. You may feel *love* for your parents and *affection* for your friend's parents.

friendship   *Friendship* is a feeling of affection, trust, and enjoyment that two or more persons have for each other. People form many *friendships* when they go to school.

fondness   *Fondness* and *liking* are feelings of
liking   enjoyment, and sometimes affection, for people or things or animals. Some people have a *fondness* for cats. You may have a *liking* for peanut butter or a *fondness* for hiking in the woods.

Donna has a **liking** for peanut butter.

devotion   *Devotion* is a very strong feeling of love either for a person or for something you believe in. Many people feel *devotion* to their country.

**love** (v)   Look up *like*.
Look up antonyms of *hate*.

**lovely**

*Lovely* is a synonym for *beautiful*, but it is a tired word. Before you use it, why not look up some other good words?

When you speak of a *lovely* picture, you might mean *beautiful* or *attractive*.

A *lovely* day is probably *sunny* or *cool* or *warm* or *clear* or *mild*.

A *lovely* child is *attractive, good, pretty, pleasant, happy, interesting, friendly,* perhaps *comical* at times.

A *lovely* time might be *delightful* or *interesting, happy, quiet, peaceful, exciting,* or *hilarious*.

A *lovely* house could be *attractive, pleasant, beautiful, comfortable, cheerful, warm,* and *peaceful*.

A *lovely* view is usually *magnificent, wonderful, delightful, thrilling,* or *calm* and *peaceful*.

A *lovely* friend is *sympathetic, kind, considerate,* perhaps *amusing,* always *interesting*.

A *lovely* party could be *delightful, exciting, gay, pleasant, enjoyable, jolly*.

A *lovely* book can be *exciting, delightful, interesting, funny, sad, scary, beautiful*.

**lurch**    Look up *walk*.

**lure**    Look up *pull*.

A worm may **lure** fish to a fishhook.

**mad** — *Mad* means without sense or self-control.

crazy
insane — A *mad* person may be *crazy* or *insane*. A *crazy* or *insane* person is sick and does not always know what he or she is doing.

angry — But *mad* is also often used to mean *angry*—greatly displeased about something. You may be *angry* because something has happened. Some people seem always to be *angry* about something, or about nothing, or just *angry* about the way things are.

annoyed
irritated
exasperated — *Annoyed, irritated, exasperated,* all mean bothered by something. Joe seemed *annoyed* because Maria had dialed the wrong number. The second time it happened, he seemed *irritated*. The third time Maria dialed the wrong number, he was *exasperated*.

fit to be tied — *Fit to be tied* is a phrase for someone who is very, very angry. When Uncle Ted couldn't find his fishing rod, he was *fit to be tied*. The fourth time Maria dialed the wrong number, Joe was *fit to be tied*.

Joe seemed **annoyed** because Maria had dialed the wrong number.

The second time it happened, he seemed **irritated.**

The third time, he seemed **exasperated.**

disgruntled
: *Disgruntled* describes someone who is in a bad mood because of something that has happened. The owner of the store tried to please a *disgruntled* customer by giving back his money.

enraged
furious
: *Enraged* and *furious* mean filled with rage or fury. An *enraged* lion tried to claw its trainer. The *furious* girl slammed her book shut and threw it down on the table.

cranky
grouchy
cross
: *Cranky, grouchy,* and *cross* describe people who feel angry most of the time. A *cranky* person becomes angry very easily, grumbles about everything, and is not pleasant to be with. A *grouchy* person complains about everything and doesn't try to get along with others. People may be *cross* and speak sharply if they are not feeling well or if something doesn't please them. Babies often are *cross* when they are sleepy. Betty will be *cross* if I am late again.

irritable
ornery
: *Irritable* and *ornery* describe people who are almost always angry or who get angry very easily. Sometimes the smallest thing will upset an *irritable* person. An *ornery* child will do the opposite of whatever anyone wants or expects.

disagreeable
: A *disagreeable* person is unpleasant and hard to get along with. A *disagreeable* smell is unpleasant and hard to put up with.

ANTONYMS: calm (adj), unruffled, pleasant, patient, peaceful, placid

The fourth time Maria dialed the wrong number, Joe was **fit to be tied.**

**magnificent**     Look up *great*.

**mail**     Look up *send*.

**majestic**     Look up *great*.

**make**     *Make* is used in many ways. It means cause something to exist or to happen. You *make* cookies. Perhaps you *made* a cake yesterday. Automobiles *have made* travel easier.

build
construct

*Build* and *construct* mean make something from materials and according to a plan. Carpenters *build* or *construct* houses. Engineers *build* or *construct* bridges. We *built* our own tree house. *Have* you ever *built* a fort? It didn't take long to *construct* this model airplane.

*Build up* can mean put something together over a period of time. You *build up* a savings account by putting a little money in the bank each week.

assemble
manufacture
put together

*Assemble, manufacture,* and *put together* mean make an object by fitting parts where they belong. Many people *assemble* or *put together* radios and toys and furniture from hobby kits. Companies *manufacture* these things by using machines that make all the parts and then *put* the parts *together*. It's fun to *put together* a banana split.

A cook may **create** a new dessert.

create
invent

*Create* and *invent* mean make something new or different from anything else. An artist may *create* a beautiful painting. A musician may *create* a great piece of music. A cook may *create* a new dessert. Many people *invent* machines that make life easier.

146

**make** continued

**establish**
**set up**

*Establish* and *set up* mean make or start something for the first time. People *establish* or *set up* rules for a new game or laws for a country. They *establish* schools and churches. Some people *set up* or *establish* funds of money to help others. Cass *set up* a dog-walking service.

**originate**

*Originate* means start a new idea or a new way of doing something. The Pilgrims *originated* Thanksgiving Day.

**fashion**
**form**

*Fashion* and *form* mean make in a certain pattern or outline. These words are often used when something is made by hand. *Fashion* may be used when someone creates one object out of another or out of unusual material. You can *fashion* a lamp out of a vase or a bottle. A shipwrecked sailor may *fashion* a sail from a shirt. A team can *form* a plan of action. The band *formed* a circle on the field.

A shipwrecked sailor may **fashion** a sail from a shirt.

**shape**

*Shape* usually means give a certain form to something. You could *shape* snow into a snowman. But you would *form* a snowman out of snow.

**force**
**compel**

*Force* and *compel* mean use power to make something happen or someone act. The door was locked, but we *forced* it open. Sometimes you have to *force* a friend to take a bath. The storm *compelled* us to go inside.

See *start* for other good words.

ANTONYMS: demolish, tear down, wreck, destroy, take apart

147

The new sidewalk was **marred** by footprints during the night.

| | |
|---|---|
| **manufacture** | Look up *make*. |
| **mar** | Look up *hurt*. |
| **march** | Look up *walk*. |
| **marvelous** | Look up *wonderful*. |
| **mask** | Look up *hide*.<br>Look up antonyms of *show*. |
| **mean** | Look up antonyms of *great* and of *kind*. |
| **melancholy** | Look up *sad*. |
| **melt** | Look up *go*. |
| **mend** | Look up antonyms of *break*. |
| **merry** | Look up *happy*.<br>Look up antonyms of *sad*. |
| **mighty** | Look up *great*. |
| **mild** | Look up *soft*.<br>Look up antonyms of *hard* and of *hot*. |
| **minor** | Look up antonyms of *important*. |
| **miserable** | Look up *sad*.<br>Look up antonyms of *happy*. |
| **mislead** | Look up *gyp*. |
| **misplace** | Look up antonyms of *find*. |
| **miss** | Look up antonyms of *catch*. |
| **mistaken** | Look up antonyms of *right*. |

The air is **misty** near a waterfall.

**misty**  Look up *dim.*

**modern**  Look up antonyms of *old.*

**moist**  Look up *wet.*

**motionless**  Look up *quiet* (adj).

**mournful**  Look up *sad.*
Look up antonyms of *happy.*

**move**  *Move* is a tired word that has many meanings. *Move* means change from one position to another or go from one place to another. Everything that lives, *moves.* That is, living things grow and change. You can *move.* You can *move* something. You can *move* somebody. You *move* when you stand up or sit down. You might *move* to another town. You can *move* your finger or your eyes. You can *move* a baby from its bed to your lap. Every kind of creature can *move.* So can things. A train or ship or a wave or a rock can *move* or *be moved.* A driver can *move* an auto or a horse. At the same time, the driver is making them *move.*

Entry words in this book that mean *move* in some way are *come* and *go, walk* and *run, fly* and *fall, pull* and *push, start, stop, shut* and *hurry, jump, put, carry, send, throw.*

You can think of many more words for *move* that are not in this book. Fish *swim,* worms *crawl,* frogs *hop,* mice *scurry,* snakes *slither,* wheels *roll,* skis *slide,* boats *float.* They all *move.*

**muffled**  Look up *dim.*

# N

| | |
|---|---|
| **narrow** | Look up *thin*. |
| **naughty** | Look up *bad*. |
| **nearly** | Look up *about*. |
| **neat** | Look up *clean*. |
| **necessary** | Look up *important*. |
| **neighbor** | Look up *friend*. |
| **net** | Look up *catch*. |

People **net** fish when they throw big nets into the water and pull them back full of fish.

| | |
|---|---|
| **new** | Look up antonyms of *old*. |
| **nibble** | Look up *eat*. |
| **nice** | *Nice* is a tired word that is often used instead of one that tells more exactly what you mean. Why not try to use another word instead of *nice*? There are many to choose from. |

A *nice* day or *nice* weather is *pleasant* or *beautiful*, *mild* or *sunny*, *warm* or *cool*, *magnificent*, *quiet*.

**150**

A *nice* person may be *friendly, attractive, beautiful, pleasant, kind, interesting, amusing, comical, quiet, patient, smart, neat.*

A *nice* time could be *happy, pleasant, peaceful, delightful, amusing, gay, exciting.*

A *nice* shirt or sweater is probably *pretty, bright, attractive, neat, appropriate, silky, soft.*

**noble**   Look up *great.*

**noise**   Everybody knows what *noise* is. A *noise* is an unpleasant sound. Here are some good words to describe different kinds or amounts of *noise.*

racket   *Racket* is a clattering noise. A carpenter driving nails or a plumber pounding on pipes can make a *racket.* The players made a great *racket* when they came down the stairs wearing their football shoes.

ruckus   *Ruckus* is noisy talk or a noisy quarrel. One loud talker can cause a *ruckus.* People who quarrel over something raise their voices and get excited enough to start a *ruckus.* Two girls started a *ruckus* over who should go first.

din   *Din* is a mixture of loud, confused noises. It is a racket that may last a long time. When you are eating in a cafeteria, sometimes it is hard to hear what the person across the table is saying because of the *din* made by dishes clattering and people talking. Traffic often makes a *din.*

**noise** continued on page 152 ◗

The players made a great **racket** when they came down the stairs wearing their football shoes.

# N

flurry

*Flurry* is a sudden short, noisy movement that breaks into a quiet place or group of people. You might cause a *flurry* if you forgot where you were and began to whistle in the library. The bridegroom caused a *flurry* when he dropped the ring.

commotion

*Commotion* means a mixture of noise and movement. It is louder and bigger than a flurry. There was a *commotion* in the room when some people started shouting at the speaker.

hubbub

*Hubbub* means loud, confused sounds or noises. It may be louder than a din. The *hubbub* was deafening when everyone talked at once.

clamor

*Clamor* is a loud noise, made by people or animals, that lasts a long time. Often a *clamor* is raised by people or animals who want something or are angry. The sheriff could not be heard above the angry *clamor* of the crowd. The animals in their cages set up a *clamor* at feeding time.

The animals in their cages set up a **clamor** at feeding time.

uproar

*Uproar* is probably the loudest noise. An *uproar* can start as a ruckus or a commotion, then grow as more people or animals join in. The audience was in an *uproar* when the rock star did not show up on time.

ANTONYMS: quiet (n), stillness

**noisy**

Look up *loud*.
Look up antonyms of *quiet* (adj).

**nudge**

Look up *push*.

He **nudged** his friend to get his attention.

O

| | |
|---|---|
| **observe** | Look up *look* and *say*. |
| **obsolete** | Look up *old*. |
| **obstruct** | Look up antonyms of *help*. |
| **obtain** | Look up *get*. |
| **occupied** | Look up antonyms of *empty*. |
| **odd** | Look up *queer*. |

**old**

*Old* describes someone who has lived for a long time or something that existed long ago. It also describes anything older than something else. Your uncle may be *old*, but not as *old* as your grandmother. If you buy a new pencil, the one you had yesterday is *old*. New and young are both antonyms of *old*.

aged
elderly

A very old person is sometimes called *aged* or *elderly*. Some people have *aged* grandparents.

ancient

*Ancient* means very old or happening long ago. People lived in caves in *ancient* times. Museums display *ancient* tools.

olden

*Olden* is often used by poets and storytellers to mean old. The *olden* days were long ago. Chief Red Cloud and Betsy Ross lived in *olden* days, but this does not mean that they lived at the same time.

obsolete

*Obsolete* means old and no longer used. Steam engines are *obsolete;* now diesel engines are used to pull trains. Years ago milk was delivered by horse and wagon. Now trucks have made milk wagons *obsolete*.

antique     *Antique* describes something that is very old but still existing and still being used. Many people use *antique* tables, chests, and chairs in their homes. *Antique* cars are valuable.

ANTONYMS: new, young, modern

**olden**     Look up *old*.

**open**     Look up *start*.
Look up antonyms of *end* (v) and of *shut*.

**operate**     Look up *run*.

**oppose**     Look up *fight*.
Look up antonyms of *help*.

**ordinary**     Look up antonyms of *wonderful* and of *queer*.

**originate**     Look up *make* and *start*.

**ornery**     Look up *mad*.

**outcome**     Look up *end* (n).

**outing**     Look up *trip* (n).

**outlandish**     Look up *queer*.

**outset**     Look up antonyms of *end* (n).

**overflowing**     Look up *full*.

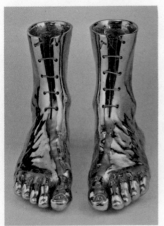

Something very odd or unusual is called **outlandish**.

# P

| | |
|---|---|
| **packed** | Look up antonyms of *empty*. |
| **pal** | Look up *friend*. |
| **parched** | Look up antonyms of *wet*. |
| **pass** | Look up *throw*. |
| **patient** | Look up antonyms of *mad*. |
| **pause** | Look up *stop*. |
| **peaceful** | Look up *quiet* (adj).<br>Look up antonyms of *mad*. |
| **peculiar** | Look up *queer*. |
| **peek** | Look up *look*. |
| **peel** | Look up *cut*. |
| **peer** | Look up *look*. |
| **peppery** | Look up *hot*. |
| **petty** | Look up antonyms of *great*. |
| **pick** | Look up *choose*. |
| **pitch** | Look up *throw*. |
| **place** | Look up *put*. |
| **placid** | Look up antonyms of *mad*. |
| **plain** | Look up antonyms of *beautiful* and of *wonderful*. |
| **plan** | Look up *think*. |
| **pleasant** | Look up *wonderful, good,* and *kind*.<br>Look up antonyms of *mad*. |
| **plump** | Look up antonyms of *thin*. |
| **plunge** | Look up *jump* and *push*. |

Laura and Curt **pitch** horseshoes at a stake.

| | |
|---|---|
| **point out** | Look up *show*. |
| **poky** | Look up antonyms of *fast* (adj). |
| **polished** | Look up *smooth*. |
| **polluted** | Look up *dirty*. Look up antonyms of *clean*. |
| **ponder** | Look up *think*. |
| **poor** | Look up *bad*. |
| **powerful** | Look up *strong*. |
| **practically** | Look up *about*. |
| **precarious** | Look up *dangerous*. |
| **precisely** | Look up antonyms of *about*. |
| **present** | Look up *show*. |
| **preserve** | Look up *keep*. |
| **pretty** | Look up *beautiful*. |
| **prevent** | Look up *stop*. |
| **problem** | Look up antonyms of *answer* (n). |
| **proceed** | Look up *go*. |
| **prod** | Look up *push*. |
| **progress** | Look up *go*. |
| **propel** | Look up *push*. |
| **proper** | Look up *right*. |
| **protect** | Look up *keep*. |
| **prove** | Look up *show*. |

Rivers and lakes are often **polluted** because garbage is dumped in the water.

# P

**pull**

*Pull* is the opposite of push. It means make an object move toward or after you. A dentist *pulls* teeth. A tractor *pulls* a plow.

*Pull* is used in many idioms. If you get a fit of giggling in class, you may *pull yourself together* and stop. Someone who tells you a wild story just to tease you is *pulling your leg.*

draw

*Draw* means pull with a steady motion and without using much strength. Knights *draw* their swords. You *drew* the curtains by pulling a cord.

drag

*Drag* means pull something along the ground. You might *drag* a heavy chair across the room if you couldn't lift it, or *drag* a log up a hill to the campfire. You might have to *drag* your dog out of the house if it is cold and rainy outside.

**Drag** means pull something along the ground.

Marcie **tugged** at the door.

haul     If you *haul* something big or heavy, you
         pull it for a long distance. Trucks *haul*
         things like logs, gravel, or automobiles.
         Freight trains even *haul* trucks.

tow      You *tow* something when you pull it along
         behind a car or boat or whatever you're
         riding in. Tugboats *tow* larger boats. Cars
         can *tow* trailers. Boats often *tow* water-skiers.

tug      You *tug* if you pull hard, sometimes
         stopping to rest between pulls. You may
         *tug* at a door that is stuck and won't open.

stretch  *Stretch* and *strain* can mean make long,
strain   steady pulls. If you *stretch* a rope from one
         tree to another, you pull it as tight as it
         will go. A dog that is tied up may *strain* at
         its leash, trying to get away.

attract  *Attract* and *lure* also mean pull, but in a
lure     different way. Something *attracts* or *lures*
         by making you want to move toward it—
         by promising something good or exciting or
         interesting. A cake *attracts* flies and draws
         them to it. A colorful cover can *attract*
         your attention to a book. Music may
         attract you to a merry-go-round. Sometimes
         the thing that *lures* is dangerous. A worm
         may *lure* fish to a fishhook. Cheese often
         *lures* a mouse into a trap.

         Antonym: push

**pure**    Look up *clean.*
            Look up antonyms of *dirty.*

**purpose** Look up *end* (n).

# P

**push**

*Push* is the opposite of pull. It means move yourself or move something by force. If you *push* a thumbtack into the bulletin board you may have to pull it out later. You *push* back your dog if it jumps on you with muddy feet. It is unpleasant to be *pushed* by someone behind you in a line.

shove

*Shove* means push roughly or carelessly. In a crowded street someone may *shove* you off the sidewalk. *Shove* also means push along on a surface. It is the opposite of drag. You can *shove* something in front of you or drag it behind you.

propel

*Propel* means make something go forward. Rockets *propel* a spaceship by pushing it through the air. The propeller on a boat *propels* it by pushing it through the water. You can *propel* a log or a raft in the water by holding onto it and kicking your feet as you would if you were swimming.

Sabrina can **propel** a raft in the water by holding onto it and kicking her feet.

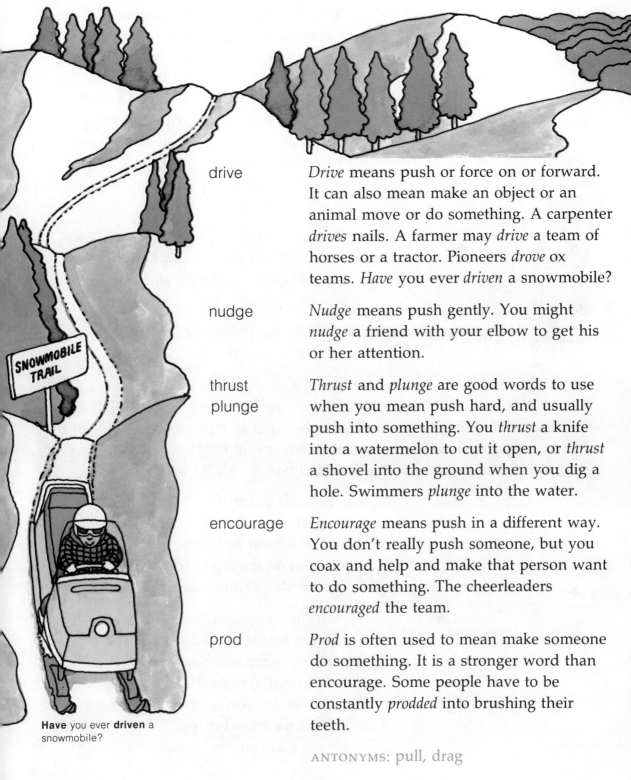

drive

*Drive* means push or force on or forward. It can also mean make an object or an animal move or do something. A carpenter *drives* nails. A farmer may *drive* a team of horses or a tractor. Pioneers *drove* ox teams. *Have* you ever *driven* a snowmobile?

nudge

*Nudge* means push gently. You might *nudge* a friend with your elbow to get his or her attention.

thrust
plunge

*Thrust* and *plunge* are good words to use when you mean push hard, and usually push into something. You *thrust* a knife into a watermelon to cut it open, or *thrust* a shovel into the ground when you dig a hole. Swimmers *plunge* into the water.

encourage

*Encourage* means push in a different way. You don't really push someone, but you coax and help and make that person want to do something. The cheerleaders *encouraged* the team.

prod

*Prod* is often used to mean make someone do something. It is a stronger word than encourage. Some people have to be constantly *prodded* into brushing their teeth.

**Have** you ever **driven** a snowmobile?

ANTONYMS: pull, drag

# P

## put

*Put* is a word that is used for many things. It really means move something to some place and leave it there. You can *put* flowers in a vase and *put* the vase on the table. Perhaps you *put* fresh flowers there yesterday, too, or *have put* them there every day all summer. You can *put* away your coat or you can *put* it on. A parent puts a baby to bed. A musician can *put* words to music.

*Put* is used in many idioms. Your class might *put on* a play. You'd better *put out* your campfire. Don't *put off* going to the dentist.

But there are other words to use for *put* that have more precise meanings.

Don't **put off** going to the dentist.

## place

*Place* means put something in a certain position. You *place* fruit in the middle of the table, or *place* chairs on each side of the table. You might *place* a heavy dish very carefully on the shelf.

## lay

*Lay* means put in a horizontal or lying-down position. You would *lay* your coat on a chair or *lay* the baby in its crib or *lay* a rug on the floor. You always have to *lay* something somewhere.

## set

*Set* means put something in a certain position for a certain purpose. You *have set* the table when you have put food and dishes on it. Ben *set* the baby in the highchair as soon as supper was ready. The doctor *sets* a broken bone. A gardener *sets out* plants in the yard.

deposit — *Deposit* means put away—you *deposit* money in the bank. If you suddenly need the money, you'll have to withdraw it. *Deposit* also means put down or drop. A heavy rain may wash sand from a hill and *deposit* it on the sidewalk.

arrange — *Arrange* means put in some order. Library books are *arranged* on the shelves in a certain way. Please *arrange* the chairs so that we can all talk together.

spread — *Spread* can be used to mean put something over or on top of something. You *spread* jelly on a piece of bread. Last fall Vi *spread* black dirt over her lawn. At the beach people often *spread* a blanket or towel to sit on.

ANTONYMS: take away, remove, withdraw

**put together** — Look up *make*.

It's fun to **put together** a banana split.

Q

**quaint**      Look up *queer*.

**quarrel**      Look up *fight* and *talk*.

**quarrelsome**      Look up antonyms of *kind*.

**queer**      *Queer* means not common, or different in some way from common, everyday things. The record sounded *queer* because it was on the wrong speed. Did you ever see such a *queer* hat?

odd      *Odd* means different from what is expected or planned. I saw an *odd* sight on the way to school. The book had an *odd* ending.

unusual      *Unusual* means different from the usual or ordinary. It was *unusual* for the class to be out so early.

strange      *Strange* means odd and hard to understand or explain. They heard a *strange* noise.

peculiar      *Peculiar* describes the looks or actions of a person which are different from everyone else's. You can say Pat has a *peculiar* walk, or you can say that kind of walk is *peculiar to* Pat. Bess has *peculiar* tastes. She likes salted marshmallows.

outlandish      *Outlandish* means something is so odd that it seems to have come from a different land. In ancient times, before people traveled very much, any stranger from a foreign country who spoke or dressed differently was an "outlander." So something very odd or unusual is still called *outlandish*.

A **quaint** street is interesting to walk along.

| | |
|---|---|
| quaint | *Quaint* means odd or different because it is old-fashioned or out of style, though it may be pretty or attractive or pleasing. A *quaint* street is interesting to walk along. |
| weird | *Weird* describes something so queer it can only be explained by supernatural or unearthly causes. We often use *weird* to describe anything odd or hard to understand. The movie about Mars had some *weird* creatures in it. |

Look up *funny* for other words to use.

ANTONYMS: common, regular, ordinary

| | |
|---|---|
| **question** (n) | Look up antonyms of *answer* (n). |
| **question** (v) | Look up antonyms of *answer* (v). |
| **quibble** | Look up *fight*. |
| **quick** | Look up *fast* (adj). |
| **quickly** | Look up *fast* (adv). |
| **quick-witted** | Look up *smart* (adj). |

# Q

**quiet** (adj)

*Quiet* is the opposite of loud. The house seemed *quiet* after the noisy children went outside. The family spent a *quiet* day at home. We always speak in *quiet* voices when we tell each other secrets.

*Quiet* also means without much movement. A sleeping kitten is *quiet.* A dog that is usually *quiet* may become restless during a thunderstorm.

silent

*Silent* means absolutely quiet, without any noise at all. The audience was *silent* as it waited for the results of the contest to be announced. Ed looked at the *silent* telephone, wishing it would ring.

still
calm
peaceful

*Still, calm,* and *peaceful* describe a gentle or hushed type of quiet. Wiggly little children are often asked to be *still.* Trees are *still* when no wind moves their leaves. On a hot summer day the lake is usually *calm* and smooth. You would speak in a *calm* voice to a small child who is lost. The country seems more *peaceful* than the busy city. Mom hopes to enjoy a *peaceful* evening when she sits down to read.

CRUNCH
CRUNCH
CRUNCH

There probably isn't a
**soundless** way to eat celery.

soundless

*Soundless* describes a complete lack of noise. There probably isn't a *soundless* way to eat potato chips or celery. A car may be *soundless* if the motor is turned off.

speechless
dumb

*Speechless* and *dumb* mean not being able to speak. Many people use *dumb* only as a synonym for stupid, but one meaning of *dumb* is *speechless.* You would probably be *speechless* if you saw an elephant at a drinking fountain. I was so nervous when I stood up to read my poem that I was *speechless*. All animals are *dumb*—except, perhaps, some birds such as parrots or parakeets. If something shocked or surprised you so much that you couldn't say a word, it struck you *dumb*.

shy     *Shy* means quiet and timid or very easily frightened. The new boy in our class is *shy*. Animals in the woods are *shy* and often frightened of humans.

tame     *Tame* describes a creature that has been trained to be obedient or gentle. It would be fun to ride a *tame* elephant. Some *tame* animals make good pets. *Tame* is the opposite of wild.

subdued     *Subdued* means not loud. The girls were noisy outside, but in class they spoke in *subdued* voices.

Some dogs are trained to stand **motionless.**

motionless     *Motionless* means without moving or unable to move. Some dogs are trained to stand *motionless*. The *motionless* fisherman waited for a fish to bite.

ANTONYMS: loud, restless, boisterous, noisy, wild, excited

**quiet** (n)     Look up antonyms of *noise*.

**quit**     Look up *stop*.

# R

| | |
|---|---|
| **race** | Look up *run*. |
| **racket** | Look up *noise*. |
| **radiant** | Look up antonyms of *dim*. |
| **ragged** | Look up *rough*. |

The nail tore a **ragged** hole in Holly's coat.

| | |
|---|---|
| **rainy** | Look up *wet*. |
| **ramble** (n) | Look up *trip* (n). |
| **ramble** (v) | Look up *go*. |
| **rapid** | Look up *fast* (adj). |
| **rapidly** | Look up *fast* (adv). |
| **receive** | Look up *get*.<br>Look up antonyms of *send*. |
| **reckless** | Look up *careless*. |
| **refuse** | Look up antonyms of *ask* and of *choose*. |
| **regular** | Look up antonyms of *queer*. |
| **reject** | Look up antonyms of *choose*. |
| **release** | Look up antonyms of *catch*. |
| **relinquish** | Look up antonyms of *get*. |
| **remain** | Look up antonyms of *run* and of *go*. |

| | |
|---|---|
| **remark** | Look up *say*. |
| **remove** | Look up antonyms of *put*. |
| **repair** | Look up antonyms of *break*. |
| **reply** (n) | Look up *answer* (n). |
| **reply** (v) | Look up *answer* (v).<br>Look up antonyms of *ask*. |
| **request** | Look up *ask*. |
| **respond** | Look up *answer* (v).<br>Look up antonyms of *ask*. |
| **response** | Look up *answer* (n). |
| **restless** | Look up antonyms of *quiet* (adj). |
| **result** | Look up *end* (n). |
| **retort** (n) | Look up *answer* (n). |
| **retort** (v) | Look up *answer* (v). |
| **retreat** | Look up *go*. |
| **reveal** | Look up *show*.<br>Look up antonyms of *hide*. |
| **ridiculous** | Look up *funny*. |

Johnny looked so **ridiculous** with pie all over his face that we had to laugh.

# R

**right**

*Right* is the opposite of wrong. When something is free from any mistake or fault, you might say it is *right.* Usually something is *right* according to certain rules or standards. Joan did the *right* thing when she apologized to her brother. But she had been wrong to laugh at him. When the teacher asked a question, Beth gave the *right* answer. Everyone must wear the *right* kind of shoes in the gym.

**correct**

*Correct* means right or true or acceptable. Dick used *correct* English in his report, but his facts were incorrect. After two false starts, we found the *correct* way to put up the tent.

**fair**
**just**

Something right or honest according to reason or a set of rules is *fair* or *just.* The judge tried to be *fair* to everyone. We think she made a *just* decision. It is *fair* for every player to have a turn. A law that is not *fair* to everyone is unjust.

**proper**
**appropriate**

If something is especially right for the time or place, it is *proper* or *appropriate.* It was *proper* for the winner to give a speech after receiving the prize. Regina's clothes were *proper* for gardening. Everyone should know the *proper* way to act at the dinner table. It is improper to talk with your mouth full. Heavy boots are *appropriate* to wear for hiking. Raincoats are usually inappropriate on sunny days. Wearing scuba gear to the dinner table would not be *appropriate.* In fact, it would not even be smart if you were very hungry!

Wearing scuba gear to the dinner table would not be **appropriate.**

**170**

**right** continued

Look up *good* for other words you might like to use instead.

ANTONYMS: wrong, incorrect, false, unjust, improper, inappropriate, mistaken

| | |
|---|---|
| **rigid** | Look up *hard*. |
| **rise** | Look up *start*. |
| | Look up antonyms of *fall*. |
| **risky** | Look up *dangerous*. |
| **roar** | Look up *laugh* and *say*. |
| **roaring** | Look up *loud*. |
| **rocky** | Look up *rough*. |
| **rope** | Look up *catch*. |

The cowhands **roped** the calf.

171

# R

**rough**

Rough is the opposite of smooth or soft. If something feels *rough*, it probably has ridges or bumps. A *rough* road is not smooth. Hand cream makes *rough* hands soft. *Rough* may also describe something that is not gentle. Soccer is a *rough* game.

Soccer is a **rough** game.

uneven
bumpy

*Uneven* and *bumpy* mean not smooth or level but having some points higher than other points. The plowed field was *uneven* and hard to walk across. You get a *bumpy* ride when you drive on a *bumpy* road.

rocky

*Rocky* means full of rocks or stones. My feet hurt from walking on the *rocky* beach.

harsh

*Harsh* is rough and without smoothness or gentleness. Sandpaper feels *harsh* if you rub your hand over it. Ruth speaks in a *harsh* voice when she is angry. The two boys said *harsh* words to each other.

rugged

*Rugged* means having a rough, uneven surface. There is much *rugged* country in the mountains. *Rugged* can also mean hard or harsh. The pioneers suffered through the rough, *rugged* winter.

172

One **scraggly** bush can spoil the looks of a neat garden.

ragged    *Ragged* means having rough or uneven edges. The nail tore a *ragged* hole in my coat.

bristly    *Bristly* is rough with short, coarse hair. My dog feels *bristly*. Dad's face feels *bristly* if he doesn't shave.

scraggly    *Scraggly* means rough or ragged and uncared for. The child's *scraggly* hair looked as if it had never been brushed. One *scraggly* bush can spoil the looks of a neat garden.

coarse    *Coarse* means rough to the touch or made up of large pieces. It is the opposite of fine. You would call a piece of cloth *coarse* if it feels rough or scratchy. One that feels smooth is fine. A beach that has *coarse* sand is not so pleasant to walk on as one with fine sand.

*Coarse* is also the opposite of delicate or dainty when it means roughly made or done. *Coarse*, heavy thread would not be used to make delicate lace. An artist can draw a flower with a few *coarse*, heavy lines of a brush or pen. She or he can also draw the same flower with delicate lines.

Look up *hard* for other words you can sometimes use instead.

ANTONYMS: smooth, soft, gentle, fine, delicate, dainty

**ruckus**    Look up *noise*.

**rugged**    Look up *rough*.

# R

**run**

*Run* means go faster than walk. You *run* to catch the school bus if you are late. Ball players *run* to a base or *run* to catch the ball. You probably *ran* somewhere yesterday. Perhaps you *have run* all the way to school when you have overslept.

*Run* can also mean move or work. Water *runs* from a faucet. A motor *runs*.

jog

*Jog* means run slowly. If you were running just for fun on a nice day, you might *jog* down the street. Athletes often *jog* along the road for exercise.

sprint

*Sprint* means run at top speed for a short distance. In a long race, a runner might *jog* along at first and then suddenly *sprint* to the finish line.

race

*Race* means move or run at the highest speed possible, usually to beat someone. If two people *race* to the corner, each one is trying to run faster than the other and to get there first. Some people *race* to answer the phone when it rings.

Some people **race** to answer the phone when it rings.

trot
lope
gallop

A horse *trots* when it moves along between a walk and a run. It *lopes* if it moves with an easy, steady stride. It *gallops* if it runs at top speed. People use these words to describe the way human beings run too. A small child walking with Dad may have to *trot* to keep up. Someone may *lope* down the street to catch a bus. Children *gallop* when they pretend they are riding horses.

bolt
chase
flee

*Bolt, chase,* and *flee* can also mean run. *Bolt* means move away suddenly. *Chase* means run fast after something. The frightened horse *bolted,* and its owner had to *chase* it. Dogs *chase* cats. People may have to *chase* their hats on a windy day. *Flee* means run away. People *flee* from a burning house. The child *fled* from the big dog. The deer *had fled* during the forest fire.

operate
work

*Operate* and *work* sometimes may be used instead of run or make something run. Factory workers *operate* machines when they run them. Many radios *operate* or *work* on batteries. Some engines *work* by steam. A wristwatch won't *work* or run if you forget to wind it.

go

*Go* can also mean run if you say your watch is *going.*

ANTONYMS: stop, remain, stay

**rush**

Look up *hurry.*

Factory workers **operate** machines.

# S

**sad**
unhappy

*Sad* is the opposite of happy. There are many other words you might use to describe how you feel when you're *unhappy* or *sad* about something.

downcast

*Downcast* really means thrown down. When you are *downcast*, you are unhappy and feel as if something were pushing you or throwing you down.

melancholy

*Melancholy* means sad and thoughtful. You may feel *melancholy* for a long time after you have lost a pet.

mournful
sorrowful

*Mournful* and *sorrowful* mean full of sadness. Lena played a *mournful* tune on her guitar. You could tell by Darrel's *sorrowful* expression that he couldn't go to the game.

sorry

*Sorry* can mean feeling sad because of something you have said or done, and wishing you had not said or done it. When you hurt someone's feelings and say you're *sorry*, you probably feel unhappy and sad. But if you accidentally step on someone's toe, or bump into someone, it is polite to say you are *sorry*. This doesn't mean you're really sad; it's simply a considerate way of excusing yourself.

miserable
wretched

If you are *miserable* or *wretched*, you are extremely unhappy about something or with something. You might feel *miserable* because you said something unkind to a friend. A cold can make you feel *miserable*. I feel *wretched* because I forgot to give you an important message.

A cold made Kenji feel
**miserable.**

**176**

forlorn

*Forlorn* means sad or lost and lonely. The *forlorn* look on the lost child's face almost brought tears to my eyes.

woebegone

*Woebegone* means looking very sorrowful. Bloodhounds always look *woebegone*.

ANTONYMS: happy, contented, cheerful, glad, merry, funny, delighted

Most people try to **save** money.

**safe**
Look up antonyms of *dangerous*.

**sail**
Look up *fly*.

**satiny**
Look up *smooth*.

**satisfied**
Look up *happy*.

**saunter**
Look up *walk*.

**save**
Look up *keep*.

**saw**
Look up *cut*.

**say**
*Say* is used so often that it has become one of the most worn-out words in our language. *Say* means put into words. You may *say* the same thing you *said* yesterday or *say* the same thing you *have said* every day for a week. *Say*, as well as many of its synonyms, can be used in two ways — with or without quotation marks: Mark *said* he was ready or Mark *said*, "I am ready."
*Say* is a good word and it should be used, but writers of stories try especially hard to find some other words to use when they write conversation between characters. There are really hundreds of words that can take the place of *say*.

**say** continued on page 178 ◗

# S

state

You *state* a fact or you *state* your opinion just by saying what you know or believe to be true about something. The police officer *stated* that we were speeding. "That is not true," Katy *stated*.

declare

You *declare* something if you say it firmly. "I won't go another step," Lula *declared*. We *declared* we had never seen anything so funny.

exclaim

You *exclaim* if you say something loudly or sharply. When I burst into the room, Grandma *exclaimed* that I had frightened her half to death. "All these letters are for you," Alex *exclaimed* impatiently. "Aha!" *exclaimed* the detective, "I have found a clue."

remark
observe
comment
agree

*Remark, observe, comment,* and *agree* may often be used for say. They all mean express an opinion in words. "Well, this has been a wonderful day," Vickie *remarked*. My neighbor *remarked* that the bus was later than usual. After Father watched us splashing in the pool for a while, he *observed* that it looked very inviting. "It's not quite four o'clock," our guide *observed*. The television announcer *commented* on the news. "That was a good ball game," *commented* Kirk. We *agreed* that the first plan was the best, even though we didn't like it. "All right, you may go," Mother *agreed*.

His neighbor **remarked** that the bus was later than usual.

| | |
|---|---|
| suggest | *Suggest* can mean offer an idea. I *suggested* that they all come along for a ride. Can you *suggest* a good place to eat? "We might take a picnic lunch to the park," *suggested* the twins. |
| begin<br>continue<br>add | *Begin, continue,* and *add* may be used for say, even though they are not really synonyms. "Once upon a time," the storyteller *began.* "After Hansel and Gretel escaped from the witch, they went on through the woods," *continued* the storyteller. "And they lived happily ever after!" *added* one child who had heard the story many times before. |
| shout<br>call | *Shout* and *call* mean say loudly. "Hurry!" Juan *shouted.* The bus driver *called,* "Last stop!" |
| scream<br>shriek<br>yell<br>roar<br>howl | *Scream, shriek, yell, roar,* and *howl,* all may be used to say something loudly or excitedly. "I want to get off," the child *screamed* as the Ferris wheel started down. We could hear *shrieks* of joy coming from the circus tent. "Popcorn. Get your popcorn here," the man *yelled.* The crowd *roared* with laughter when fifteen clowns got out of one little car. "Someone sat on my cotton candy!" Patrick *howled* at the top of his lungs. |

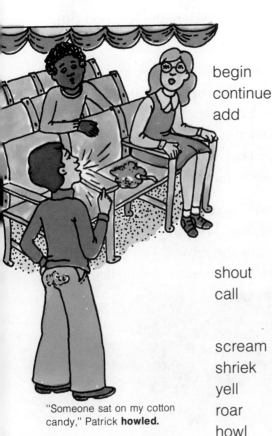

"Someone sat on my cotton candy," Patrick **howled.**

Look up *talk* for other words to use.

| | |
|---|---|
| **scanty** | Look up *little.* |

# S

**scare**
*Scare* means cause sudden fear. It is sometimes hard to calm someone who has been *scared*. Did the loud noise *scare* you? My sister *scared* me when she jumped out from behind the couch.

alarm
*Alarm* means warn of approaching danger. Sometimes it means upset someone with the thought of danger. The siren will probably *alarm* the townspeople. I don't wish to *alarm* you, but we may have a flood if this rain continues another day.

frighten
*Frighten* means scare. The clap of thunder *frightened* the dog. We put up a scarecrow to *frighten* away the crows. The small child was *frightened* by the monster masks.

The small child was **frightened** by the monster masks.

terrify
*Terrify* means frighten or fill with terror. The huge bear *terrified* the campers when it came toward them out of the woods. We were so *terrified* by the weird noise that we couldn't move.

ANTONYMS: calm (v), soothe

**scared**
Look up *afraid.*

**180**

| | |
|---|---|
| **scary** | If something scares you, you'd probably say it was *scary*. *Scary* is a perfectly good word, but there are others you can use too. |
| frightening | *Frightening* means scary. The owl's screech outside our tent was really *frightening*. |
| spooky | *Spooky* means scary because you think ghosts may appear any moment. We saw a *spooky* movie. It was *spooky* in the old deserted mansion. |
| terrifying<br>horrifying | *Terrifying* and *horrifying* are strong words meaning scary. A *terrifying* noise or a *horrifying* sight fills you with great fear. |

The child's **scraggly** hair looked as if it had never been brushed.

| | |
|---|---|
| **scraggly** | Look up *rough*. |
| **scream** | Look up *say* and *shout*. |
| **see** | Look up *look*. |
| **seize** | Look up *catch*. |
| **select** | Look up *choose*. |
| **send** | *Send* means make something or someone move from where you are to some other place. Some people *send* their clothes to a laundry. The principal *sent* me on an errand. Scientists *have sent* rockets into outer space. |
| mail | *Mail* means send a package or letter to the post office so that it may be delivered tc the person you are sending it to. You can *mail* your letter at the corner mailbox. |

**send** continued on page 182 ▶

ship

*Ship* means put something aboard a ship or plane or some other vehicle to send it from one place to another. You'd *ship* a trunk or mail a package.

transmit

*Transmit* means send from one place or person to another. It also means send out signals. If you will *transmit* the message to me, I will send it on. Sailors *transmit* storm warnings by radio.

dispatch

*Dispatch* means send off or away. The king *dispatched* a messenger with a note for the queen. Some people *dispatch* messages by sending a carrier pigeon that will fly straight to its home loft with a message tied to its leg.

Some people **dispatch** messages by carrier pigeons.

Look up *carry* for other words you might use.

ANTONYMS: receive, get

**set**　　　　　Look up *put*.

**set up**　　　Look up *make*.

**severe**　　　Look up *awful, bad,* and *hard*.

**shadowy**　　Look up *dim*.

**shady**　　　Look up *dim*.
　　　　　　　Look up antonyms of *bright*.

**shape**　　　Look up *make*.

**shatter**　　Look up *break*.

**shiny**　　　Look up *bright*.
　　　　　　　Look up antonyms of *dim*.

**ship**　　　　Look up *send*.

**shoot**　　　Look up *throw*.

Basketball players **shoot** baskets.

182

The children **shrieked** as they started downhill on the roller coaster.

**shout**

*Shout* means cry out loudly. It's the opposite of whisper. When you cry out or *shout*, you probably say words or sentences that can be understood. You might *shout* to a friend across the street. People often *shout* at each other if they lose their tempers. You have to *shout* when you talk to a person who can't hear well.

call

*Call* means make a sound with your voice in order to get someone's attention — *call* for help or *call* your dog. "Wait a minute," Robin *called* from the doorway. "Hurry back!" they *called* as we drove away. Melba *called* to me from the window.

scream
shriek
yell

If you *scream* or *shriek* or *yell*, you call out at the top of your lungs. You might say words, but you probably would just make a long, loud sound. Nora *screamed* with delight when she saw the newborn pony. We *shrieked* as we started downhill on the roller coaster. Mr. Ling *yelled* at us when we ran into the street.

yodel

*Yodel* is a special way to shout. It is done by shifting your voice back and forth from a very high note to your regular voice, making a kind of wavering sound. People living in the mountains often *yodel*, and the sound echoes from peak to peak.

Look up *say* to see if some other words would better fit what you mean.

ANTONYM: whisper

**shove**

Look up *push*.

183

# S

**show**

*Show* means be seen or let something be seen. Happiness or sadness may *show* on a person's face. You may *show* anger even though you try to hide it or mask it with a smile. A baby's actions may *show* that he is ready for a nap.

**point out**

*Point out* is an idiom that means show something which has not been seen or understood before. In a strange city someone might *point out* the most interesting sights.

**present**
**display**

*Present* and *display* can be used when someone is showing objects to people. Stores *present* the latest fashions. A theater *presents* a movie. Storekeepers *display* their goods so customers will know what is for sale. They often *display* objects in their windows.

**exhibit**

*Exhibit* means show something publicly. Artists *exhibit* their work in galleries and at art fairs.

Artists **exhibit** their work.

**184**

demonstrate

*Demonstrate* means show how something is done. A Scout leader builds a fire to *demonstrate* how it is done. A coach might use movies to point out what the players are doing wrong, then *demonstrate* the correct way.

direct
lead
guide

*Direct*, *lead*, and *guide* mean show or help someone find the way to wherever that person is going. Police officers *direct* traffic. A police officer would *direct* you to a place you want to go, but would not go with you. If you *lead* a group of people, you usually go ahead of them. If you *have led* a horse, you held it by a strap or rope. You *guide* people when you know all the places where they might have trouble or get lost and you help them get past these places safely. A firefighter would *lead* people out of a burning building, and would *guide* them down a ladder.

Police officers **direct** traffic.

reveal

*Reveal* means show plainly or make known something that has been concealed or should be hidden. A flashlight's beam *reveals* the inside of a cave. Some people *reveal* secrets.

prove

*Prove* means show that something is true by finding and pointing out facts. When you disagree with someone, you can *prove* your point by finding facts that show you are right. You may have *proved* that you are able to run faster than anyone in your class by winning a race.

ANTONYMS: hide, mask, conceal

# S

**shriek**    Look up *say* and *shout*.

**shrill**    Look up *loud*.

**shuffle**    Look up *walk*.

By the time Jules **had shut** the door, the floor was covered with snow.

**shut**

*Shut* means move into place so that there is no opening or so that nothing can go through or past. You *shut* a door or window to keep cold air out. Perhaps yesterday you *shut* it too. You could *have shut* it twice today. A cat *shuts* its eyes to keep out the light. By the time Jules *had shut* the door, the floor was covered with snow.

*Shut off* and *shut out* are idioms. You *shut off* the water when you turn a faucet off. You pull down a shade to *shut out* the sunshine. A pile of rocks *had shut off* our only path to freedom.

close

*Close* is the opposite of open. *Close* means shut off an opening or passage or end something. The city may *close* the road for repairs. After I took out my socks I *closed* the drawer. The circus *closes* today. You *close* something by bringing two ends or sides together, or maybe by lowering a lid. *Close* the book. She pulled a zipper to *close* her jacket.

They were glad the angry gorilla was **imprisoned** within its cage.

slam

*Slam* means shut by using force or by making a loud noise. A door *slams* if the wind pushes it shut very hard and fast. An angry person may *slam* a drawer shut or *slam* down the cover of a box.

bar

*Bar* means shut out by putting a bar across an opening. Pioneers *barred* the doors of their cabins. You *bar* the gate to keep horses in a corral.

block

*Block* means shut off or hinder someone from going forward. A big truck *blocked* the road. The giant standing in the path *blocked* their way.

imprison

*Imprison* means shut in so that no escape is possible. We were glad the angry gorilla was *imprisoned* within its cage.

Look up *stop* for other words you might want to use.

ANTONYMS: open, unfasten

**shy**      Look up *quiet* (adj).

**silent**   Look up *quiet* (adj).
             Look up antonyms of *loud*.

**silky**    Look up *smooth*.

**silly**    Look up *stupid*.

**simple**   Look up antonyms of *hard*.

**sink**     Look up *fall*.

# S

Many athletes **skip** rope.

| | |
|---|---|
| **sizzling** | Look up *hot.* |
| **skilled** | Look up *good.* |
| **skim** | Look up *fly.* |
| **skimpy** | Look up *little.* |
| **skinny** | Look up *thin.* |
| **skip** | Look up *jump.* |
| **slam** | Look up *shut.* |
| **slash** | Look up *cut.* |
| **sleek** | Look up *smooth.* |
| **slender** | Look up *thin.* |
| **slice** | Look up *cut.* |
| **slick** | Look up *smooth.* |
| **slim** | Look up *thin.* |
| **slippery** | Look up *smooth.* |
| **slit** | Look up *cut.* |
| **sloppy** | Look up *careless* and *wet.* |
| **slow** (adj) | Look up antonyms of *fast* (adj). |
| **slow** (adv) | Look up antonyms of *fast* (adv). |
| **slow down** | Look up antonyms of *hurry.* |
| **slowly** | Look up antonyms of *fast* (adv). |
| **sluggish** | Look up antonyms of *fast* (adj). |
| **sluggishly** | Look up antonyms of *fast* (adv). |
| **small** | Look up *little.* |
| | Look up antonyms of *large* and of *great.* |

The **smart** pup figured out how to open the gate.

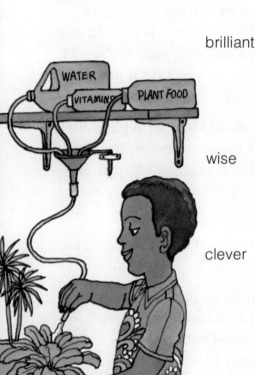

George invented a **clever** way to water his plants.

**smart** (adj)    *Smart* means able to learn easily and to understand and solve problems quickly. It is the opposite of stupid. The *smart* pup figured out how to open the gate. Lucy is a *smart* girl; her science project is good.

intelligent    *Intelligent* means smart and able to think clearly, understand, and make good decisions. But even an *intelligent* person sometimes makes a dumb mistake.

bright    *Bright* is often used to mean smart. Then it is the opposite of dull. It was a *bright* idea to build a clubhouse.

brilliant    *Brilliant* is a stronger word than bright. Something or someone very outstanding is called *brilliant*. Cindy made some *brilliant* remarks at the meeting. Victor is a *brilliant* pianist.

wise    *Wise* means able to understand people and able to understand things that happen. A *wise* person usually knows how to deal with problems.

clever    *Clever* means quick to think of something or skillful at doing something. The *clever* boy had a plan for an American Indian Day program. Jean is *clever* at making belt buckles. George invented a *clever* way to water his plants while he is on vacation.

quick-witted    *Quick-witted* means quick to think and understand. A *quick-witted* person may guess a riddle fast. A dim-witted person may never guess it.

ANTONYMS: stupid, dumb, dull, dim-witted

189

**Smeared** often means dirty because of careless handling.

| | |
|---|---|
| **smart** (v) | Look up *hurt*. |
| **smash** | Look up *break*. |
| **smeared** | Look up *dirty*. |
| **smile** | Look up *laugh*. |
| **smoky** | Look up *dim*. |

**smooth**
*Smooth* is the opposite of rough and bumpy. *Smooth* means having a surface without high and low points. A lake is *smooth* when there are no ripples or waves.

even
Something is *even* if it is regular and smooth. An *even* sidewalk is easy to skate on. An uneven sidewalk may be bumpy. People with *even* tempers do not get angry very often.

level
flat
*Level* and *flat* mean having no parts higher or lower than the rest. The recipe called for a *level* teaspoonful of sugar. Airplanes need *level* ground to land on. A hockey rink should be *flat*.

polished
*Polished* means smooth and shiny. *Polished* furniture is smooth to the touch.

slippery
*Slippery* describes something so smooth it is hard to hold on to. Ice is *slippery* to walk on. A tool covered with oil or grease is *slippery* and hard to hold.

slick
sleek
*Slick* and *sleek* both mean smooth. *Slick* usually refers to a smooth surface. A *slick* pond is good for skating. *Sleek* has the added meaning of glossy. A dog or a cat or a horse has a *sleek* coat if its hair is smooth and shiny.

creamy

*Creamy* means like cream, which is smooth. Fudge is *creamy* candy. It feels *creamy* and smooth in your mouth, if it doesn't have nuts in it.

silky
satiny
velvety

*Silky, satiny, velvety,* all describe some surface that feels or looks as smooth as silk or satin or velvet. Something *velvety* is smooth and soft. Hair is often called *silky.* A leaf might be *satiny.* A rose petal is *velvety.*

Look up *soft* for other words to use.

ANTONYMS: rough, bumpy, uneven, wrinkled

It is hard to walk in **soft** mud.

**smudged**    Look up *dirty.*

**snatch**    Look up *catch.*

**snicker**    Look up *laugh.*

**snip**    Look up *cut.*

**soaking**    Look up *wet.*

**soar**    Look up *fly.*

**soft**    *Soft* means not hard or rough or severe. A baby's skin is *soft.* Pudding is *soft.* Silk, satin, and velvet are *soft* to the touch; burlap is coarse and rough. On a summer evening the air feels *soft.* An icy wind feels harsh. It is easy to walk on firm ground, but hard to walk in *soft* mud.

*Soft* may also mean not loud. A person with a *soft* voice does not speak roughly or too loud.

**soft** continued on page 192 ▸

Be **gentle** with newborn kittens.

fleecy

*Fleecy* means soft like sheep's wool. We call big, white, soft-looking clouds *fleecy*. A *fleecy* blanket feels good on a cold night.

fluffy

*Fluffy* means soft and light. Mashed potatoes should be *fluffy*. I like a *fluffy* pillow on my bed.

mild
gentle

*Mild* and *gentle* mean not hard or rough. A *mild* climate never gets too hot or too cold. A *mild* person does not get angry very often. Be *gentle* with newborn puppies and kittens. Grandpa gave me a *gentle* pat on the head.

lenient

*Lenient* means not harsh or stern. I was too *lenient* when I let the dog play with my slippers — now she plays with all my shoes. I should have been more firm.

Look up *smooth* for other words that might be better for what you want to say.

ANTONYMS: hard, rough, loud, coarse, harsh, firm, stern

**soggy**      Look up *wet*.

**soiled**     Look up *dirty*.
Look up antonyms of *clean*.

**solid**      Look up *hard*.

**solution**   Look up *answer* (n).

**solve**      Look up *answer* (v).

**soothe**     Look up antonyms of *scare*.

**sorrowful**  Look up *sad*.
Look up antonyms of *happy*.

| | |
|---|---|
| **sorry** | Look up *sad*. |
| **soundless** | Look up *quiet* (adj). |
| **sparkling** | Look up *bright*. |
| **speak** | Look up *talk*. |
| **spectacular** | Look up *wonderful*. |
| **speechless** | Look up *quiet* (adj). |
| **speed** | Look up *hurry*. |
| **speedily** | Look up *fast* (adv). |
| **speedy** | Look up *fast* (adj). |
| **spick-and-span** | Look up *clean*. Look up antonyms of *dirty*. |
| **splendid** | Look up *wonderful*. |
| **split** | Look up *break*. |
| **spoil** | Look up *hurt*. |
| **spoiled** | Look up *bad*. |
| **spooky** | Look up *scary*. |
| **spotless** | Look up *clean*. |
| **spotted** | Look up *dirty*. |
| **spread** | Look up *put*. |
| **spring** | Look up *start* and *jump*. |
| **sprint** | Look up *run*. |
| **squabble** | Look up *fight*. |
| **stagger** | Look up *walk*. |
| **stained** | Look up *dirty*. |

Sandy **staggered** when she got off the merry-go-round.

# S

**stalk**       Look up *walk*.

**stare**       Look up *look*.

**start**

*Start* is the opposite of stop. When you make the first movement from a still position, you *start*. Also, if you turn on a machine, you *start* it. You *start* on a trip when you leave home. Runners in a race *start* when the gun goes off. A gun *starts* the race.

*Start* also means do something for the first time or cause something to exist. We *started* going to the swimming pool in June. A river *starts* from a tiny stream. A group of students can *start* a newspaper.

Other words are better to use than *start* for some of these meanings.

begin

*Begin* means start something that may go on for some time. If you *begin* something you usually try to finish it. But something that *begins* usually ends. For example, you *begin* a book. When you have read it all, you have finished it. The story *begins* with their arrival in the city. Julie *began* to write a letter. It *has begun* to rain again.

open

*Open* can mean start or begin something. A person can *open* a new store. If business is bad, he or she may close it soon. A new play *opens* at a theater. A show may *open* with a magician's act or with acrobats. It may conclude, or end, with a big, colorful dance number.

Plants **spring** from seeds.

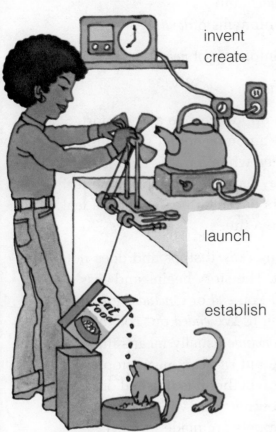

A person may **invent** a machine or something that is useful.

**start** continued

rise
spring
originate

*Rise, spring,* and *originate* mean start or come into being from something else. Some rivers *rise* from mountain streams. Plants *spring* from seeds. Moccasins worn today *originated* from the soft shoes made by the Algonquin Indians.

introduce

You *introduce,* or start, something when you bring it to the attention of people who did not know or think about it before. The girls *introduced* a new style when they wore socks of different colors. You *introduce* strangers to each other.

invent
create

*Invent* and *create* can mean start or make something that has never been made before. A person may *invent* a machine or something that is useful. Paper was *invented* a long time ago by Ts'ai Lun, a Chinese government worker. A person may *create* something just for the sake of beauty. A statue or painting is *created* by a sculptor or an artist.

launch

To *launch* a boat you put it into the water for the first time. You also *launch* a program or a project by starting it.

establish

*Establish* means start some new idea or custom or thing. People *establish* schools and churches. A new city would *establish* a new government. Dorothy Eustice *established* Seeing-Eye dog training schools.

Look up *make* for other words to use.

ANTONYMS: stop, finish, end (v), close, conclude

195

# S

| | |
|---|---|
| **state** | Look up *say*. |
| **stately** | Look up *great*. |
| **stay** | Look up antonyms of *run* and of *go*. |
| **steaming** | Look up *hot*. |
| **step** | Look up *walk*. |
| **stern** | Look up *hard*. Look up antonyms of *soft*. |
| **stiff** | Look up *hard*. |
| **still** | Look up *quiet* (adj). Look up antonyms of *loud*. |
| **stillness** | Look up antonyms of *noise*. |
| **sting** | Look up *hurt*. |

**stop**      *Stop* is the opposite of go and of start. *Stop* means not go on or not let something go on. Cars *stop* when a traffic light is red. An umpire may have to *stop* an argument that two players have started. You *stop* a leak in a roof or in a tire.

end
conclude      If something *ends,* it stops and does not start again. The story begins and *ends* on the desert. You *end* or *conclude* something by stopping it. We *ended* our conversation quickly. *Conclude* usually means finish something, but *end* can mean stop something whether it is finished or not. The puppet show *concluded* with a demonstration of how puppets are made to move.

The puppet show **concluded** with a demonstration of how puppets are made to move.

cease      *Cease* can mean stop or come to an end gradually. The ticking of our clock got slower and slower; then it *ceased*.

pause

You *pause* if you stop doing something for a minute or two and then continue. As we passed the store, we *paused* to look in the windows. The speaker *paused* to take a drink of water, then went on speaking.

discontinue

If you stop something you have been doing regularly, you *discontinue* it. The school cafeteria *discontinued* serving lunch. We forgot to *discontinue* the newspaper and milk deliveries before we went away.

quit

*Quit* means stop or give up something. You can *quit* a job or *quit* taking music lessons or *quit* biting your fingernails. They *quit* talking when the movie began. It's about time that your sister *has quit* teasing you.

halt

*Halt* usually means stop or bring to a stop. The band marched across the field and then *halted*. The police ordered the fleeing robber to *halt*.

prevent

*Prevent* means stop something from moving or happening. Ropes *prevented* the crowd from getting too close to the parade.

arrest

*Arrest* means stop or capture. The sheriff *arrested* the rustlers and took them to jail. A cloud of smoke coming from a building may *arrest* your attention as you pass by. *Arrest* also means bring to a stop or slow down. Doctors tried to *arrest* the infection.

You may find better words for what you want to say if you look up *end* (v) and *shut*.

The speaker **paused** to take a drink of water, then went on speaking.

ANTONYMS: go, start, begin, continue

# S

| | |
|---|---|
| **stout** | Look up *strong*. |
| | Look up antonyms of *thin*. |
| **strain** | Look up *pull*. |
| **strange** | Look up *queer*. |
| **stray** | Look up *go*. |
| **stretch** | Look up *pull*. |
| **stride** | Look up *walk*. |
| **stroll** | Look up *walk*. |

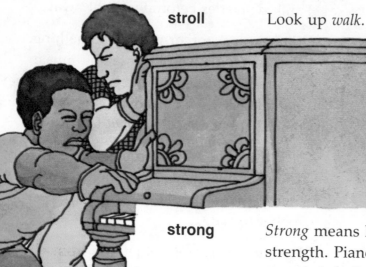

Piano movers have to be very **strong**.

**strong**    *Strong* means having great power or strength. Piano movers have to be very *strong*. A frail mover could not lift anything so heavy. Grandmother likes to drink *strong* tea, but Dad likes weak tea.

stout    *Stout* sometimes means brave and strong. The mountain climbers had *stout* hearts; they struggled on to the top. *Stout* also means firm. A *stout* stick helps you walk over rough ground. You need a *stout* ladder to reach the roof.

sturdy    *Sturdy* means strong and firm. That *sturdy* tree has lived through many windstorms. A *sturdy* box is well-made. One that is not well-made is flimsy.

**198**

tough | *Tough* means firm and strong and able to resist wear and tear. Shoes made of *tough* leather will last a long time. A *tough* boxer can take lots of punches. *Tough* meat is hard to chew.

forceful | *Forceful* means full of strength or force. The speaker had a *forceful* manner. His voice was not weak or feeble. A *forceful* wind tore at the TV antenna.

powerful | *Powerful* means full of strength and power. The *powerful* tractor pulled the big truck out of the ditch. An elephant is *powerful* enough to push a tree out of the ground.

An elephant is **powerful** enough to push a tree out of the ground.

hardy | *Hardy* means strong and healthy and able to stand up against difficult things. The girl is *hardy* now, but she was frail when she was a baby. A *hardy* plant can live through very cold weather.

ANTONYMS: weak, frail, flimsy, feeble

**stuffed** | Look up *full.*

**stumble** | Look up *walk.*

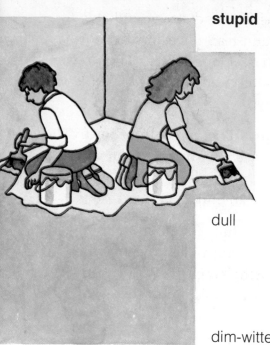

Norman and Jenny felt **dim-witted** when they painted themselves into a corner.

**stupid**

*Stupid* means very slow to understand and learn. I felt *stupid* when I couldn't do the math problem. Something without sense can also be called *stupid*. People who are very smart sometimes do or say *stupid* things. Although she came up with a brilliant idea, some people thought it was *stupid*. It seemed as if the *stupid* play would never end.

dull

*Dull* can mean slow in thinking or learning or acting. Some people are *dull* when they first wake up. When something is not interesting, it is *dull* and uninteresting. Some TV programs are *dull*.

dim-witted

*Dim-witted* means not thinking clearly. You'd feel pretty *dim-witted* if you painted yourself into a corner.

dumb

*Dumb* really means unable to speak. But it is often used in place of stupid, especially to describe someone who can't say what he or she means. Your sudden temper tantrum left me *dumb*—with nothing to say. My answer to your surprising question must have sounded pretty *dumb*.

silly
foolish
crazy

*Silly, foolish,* and *crazy* mean without sense or thought. What a *silly* thing to say! People who giggle all the time sound *silly*. It was *foolish* to go without a coat on such a cold day. He made a *foolish* mistake. Riding your bike on the wrong side of the road is a *crazy* thing to do.

| | |
|---|---|
| **sturdy** | Look up *strong*. |
| **subdued** | Look up *quiet* (adj). |
| | Look up antonyms of *loud*. |
| **sudden** | Look up *fast* (adj). |
| **suddenly** | Look up *fast* (adv). |
| **suggest** | Look up *say*. |
| **sultry** | Look up *hot*. |
| **sunny** | Look up *bright*. |
| **superb** | Look up *wonderful*. |
| **support** | Look up *help*. |
| **suppose** | Look up *think*. |
| **sweltering** | Look up *hot*. |
| | Look up antonyms of *cold*. |

The dog came to a **sudden** stop when it was called.

On a **sweltering** day Liz just wants to sit in the shade of a tree.

| | |
|---|---|
| **swift** | Look up *fast* (adj). |
| **swiftly** | Look up *fast* (adv). |
| **swindle** | Look up *gyp*. |
| **sympathetic** | Look up *kind*. |

# T

| | |
|---|---|
| **tactful** | Look up *kind*. |
| **take** | Look up *carry*. |
| **take apart** | Look up antonyms of *make*. |
| **take away** | Look up antonyms of *put*. |
| **take off** | Look up *go*. |

**talk**

*Talk* means express a thought or share ideas with someone by using your voice and forming words. *Talk* usually suggests that you say words to someone who listens to you and then replies. People *talk* to each other.

But it is possible to *talk* to someone or to something that does not listen or reply. You can *talk* to your dog or *talk* to yourself or *talk* to a baby. You can also *talk* to a group of people. The fire chief *talked* to our class about fire prevention. You *talk* to someone or something. You *talk* about something—about the weather or about a vacation.

It is possible to **talk** to someone who does not listen.

**speak**

*Speak* means say words whether you're talking to someone or not. Perhaps you *spoke* to your pet turtle. You may *have spoken* to someone who didn't hear you. You can *speak* fast or *speak* loudly. Some people *speak* several languages. You *speak* to friends if you say "Hi" when you meet them on the street. Maybe you both stop and talk, or maybe you go right on.

tell

*Tell* usually means give information to someone by speaking. You might *tell* your little sister the same bedtime story you *told* the night before. Perhaps you *have told* the same story many times because she likes it so much.

chat
gossip

*Chat* and *gossip* mean talk about something interesting but usually not very important. Perhaps you *chat* with a friend every evening over the telephone. You *gossip* if you talk about somebody or tell secrets that friends have trusted you not to tell.

comment

*Comment* means tell what you think about something. You might *comment* on a friend's new shoes, on a book you have read, or on how nice someone looks.

discuss

*Discuss* means talk about some subject and think about all sides of a question. The class *discussed* plans for our spring clean-up project. We *discussed* the problem of finding a safe place to skate.

argue
dispute
quarrel

*Argue, dispute,* and *quarrel* mean not just discuss, but disagree. These are strong words. Don't *argue* with the umpire. You *argue* with your brother when you tell him all the reasons why you are right and he is wrong. When he *argues* back, you *dispute* everything he says, and probably you both get angry enough to *quarrel*. If you are *quarreling,* you are fighting with words.

Look up *say* for other words you might use.

Don't **argue** with the umpire.

**203**

# T

| | |
|---|---|
| **tame** | Look up *quiet* (adj). |
| **tear** | Look up *break*. |
| **tear down** | Look up antonyms of *make*. |
| **tell** | Look up *talk*. |
| **tend** | Look up *keep*. |
| **tender** | Look up antonyms of *hard*. |
| **tepid** | Look up *hot*. |
| **terrible** | Look up *awful*. |
| **terrified** | Look up *afraid*. |
| **terrify** | Look up *scare*. |
| **terrifying** | Look up *scary*. |
| **thick** | Look up antonyms of *thin*. |

**thin**  *Thin* describes something that is not thick or that is small as you measure it from side to side. *Thin* ice is dangerous. *Thin* paper is easy to trace through. People often have thick hair when they are young, but their hair becomes *thin* as they grow older. You can draw a *thin* line or a heavy, thick line. A person who is not *thin* may be called stout, plump, or heavy.

lean
skinny  *Lean* and *skinny* mean not fat. *Lean* meat does not have much fat. A thin person is *lean,* but a very thin person may be called *skinny.* But no one would ask for a piece of *skinny* meat.

**Lean** and **skinny** mean not fat.

**204**

slender
slim

*Slender* and *slim* describe something that is narrower than it is long or tall. Flowers have *slender* stems. Usually *slender* and *slim* describe thin people. *Slim* can also mean small. We have a *slim* chance of winning the game. A *slim* package is easier to carry than a bulky one.

A **slim** package is easier to carry than a bulky one.

fine

*Fine* means thin or slender. *Fine* thread might be no thicker than a hair, but coarse thread is almost as thick as string. A baby's hairbrush has *fine* bristles. *Fine* wire is good for hanging small pictures. But you would need heavy or stout wire for hanging big pictures.

narrow

*Narrow* means not wide or far across. A *narrow* street has very little room for cars to pass each other.

ANTONYMS: thick, heavy, stout, plump, fat, bulky, coarse, wide, broad

205

# T

**think**

*Think* means use your mind to form a thought or an idea. The scientist *thought* about the problem until she finally found an answer. She *had thought* about it for a long time.

Here are some good words to use for different ways to *think*.

believe
suppose
imagine

*Believe, suppose,* and *imagine* mean think that something is true. You may not be able to prove it, but you form an opinion about it from whatever facts you do have.

*Believe* is the strongest of these three words. If you *believe* in some idea, you feel strongly that that idea is right and true. You may *believe* there is life on other planets. For a long time people *believed* the earth was flat.

If you *suppose* or *imagine* something is true, you think it probably is true because it seems to be and no one has proved that it isn't. You may *suppose* a story is true because you read it in the newspaper. You *imagine* that it will rain if black clouds cover the sky.

Diane tried to **guess** how fast the car was going as it was passing the house.

wonder

*Wonder* means think about something when you don't know for sure what is true. You *wonder* what kind of work you will do when you grow up. You *wonder* what it feels like to be a butterfly.

guess

*Guess* means make up your mind about something without having any facts to base your opinion on. You might *guess* how fast a car is going as it passes the house.

consider  
ponder  

*Consider* and *ponder* mean think about something very seriously and very hard. If you had something very important to do or decide, you would *consider* it carefully and for quite a while. You might *ponder* it for several days before making up your mind.

plan  

*Plan* means think about something you are going to do and arrange all the steps or parts in order. A family *plans* a vacation by deciding when and where to go, how to get there, and what to take along.

A family **plans** a vacation by deciding when and where to go, how to get there, and what to take along.

**thoughtful**  Look up *kind*.  
Look up antonyms of *careless*.

**thoughtless**  Look up *careless*.

**thrilling**  Look up *interesting*.

# T

**throw**

*Throw* means make something go through the air by moving the arm and hand in a certain way. Let's *throw* darts at a target. Who *threw* this cap on the table? The children *have thrown* their coats on a chair. There are different ways to *throw*.

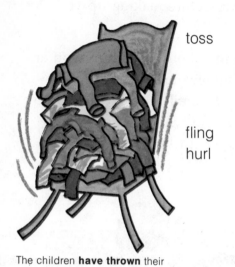

The children **have thrown** their coats on a chair.

toss

*Toss* means throw very lightly or easily. You would *toss* a beachball to another person or *toss* an eraser to someone sitting near you.

fling
hurl

*Fling* and *hurl* mean throw something hard without caring just where it goes. If you make a mistake while writing a letter, you might crumple the paper and *fling* it at the wastebasket. The baby *flung* a cup to the floor. You would *hurl* something that is heavy. The giant picked up a rock and *hurled* it down the mountainside.

pitch

You *pitch* something when you aim carefully and try to hit a certain spot. You might *pitch* snowballs at a tree just for fun. *Pitch* may be used to mean throw in some games. A pitcher *pitches* by throwing the baseball over the plate. You *pitch* horseshoes at a stake.

shoot
pass

*Shoot* and *pass* also are used to mean throw in some games. Basketball players *shoot* baskets by throwing the basketball through the hoop. A star player *has shot* many baskets. A football player *passes* by throwing the football to another team member.

The people were afraid the chimney would **topple.**

| | |
|---|---|
| **throw away** | Look up antonyms of *keep*. |
| **thrust** | Look up *push*. |
| **thunderous** | Look up *loud*. |
| **timid** | Look up *afraid*. Look up antonyms of *brave*. |
| **tiny** | Look up *little*. Look up antonyms of *large*. |
| **tip** | Look up *end* (n). |
| **tiptoe** | Look up *walk*. |
| **topple** | Look up *fall*. |
| **torrid** | Look up *hot*. Look up antonyms of *cold*. |
| **toss** | Look up *throw*. |
| **tote** | Look up *carry*. |
| **tough** | Look up *strong* and *hard*. |
| **tour** | Look up *trip* (n). |
| **tow** | Look up *pull*. |
| **transmit** | Look up *send*. |
| **transport** | Look up *carry*. |
| **trap** | Look up *catch*. |
| **travel** (n) | Look up *trip* (n). |
| **travel** (v) | Look up *go*. |
| **tremendous** | Look up *great*. |
| **trick** | Look up *gyp*. |

Boats often **tow** water-skiers.

# T

**trip** (n)

A *trip* is the act of going from where you are to somewhere else. There are many kinds of *trips* and many words to use for them.

travel

*Travel* is a word that means any kind of going from place to place. You may speak of air *travel*. You may read about the *travels* of someone. *Travel* may be a hobby for some people.

**Travel** may be a hobby for some people.

journey

*Journey* means a trip from one place to another. Even the word itself has traveled a long way. Long ago the French word for "day" became "jour," and "journée" meant "a day's travel." We borrowed the word, and now the English word *journey* means a trip, even though it may take longer than a day to complete.

tour

If you take a *tour,* you go on a trip, stopping at several places before the *tour* is finished. Some *tours* end at the place from which they started.

voyage

A *voyage* is usually a long trip by ship. Going to Africa on an ocean liner is a *voyage.*

cruise

A *cruise* is a voyage that takes you to several places. You would visit several cities on a Great Lakes *cruise.*

flight

A *flight* is a trip by air. On a tour of the United States you would probably take several *flights.*

expedition

An *expedition* is a trip for some special purpose. Explorers have gone on *expeditions* to the South Pole to learn more

Scientists go on **expeditions** to find ancient buried cities.

about the earth. Scientists go on *expeditions* to find ancient buried cities. You may go on a shopping *expedition* to buy supplies before school begins.

| | |
|---|---|
| excursion<br>jaunt | An *excursion* and a *jaunt* are short trips just for fun. Perhaps you take a *jaunt* to the beach or to the country some weekend. An *excursion* to the city or to the mountains may be a good trip for a short vacation. |
| outing | An *outing* is an excursion, sometimes with a picnic lunch outdoors. Your class may plan an *outing* at a farm. |
| ramble | A *ramble* is usually a walk going nowhere in particular. Today was perfect for a *ramble* in the park. |
| **trip** (v) | Look up *walk*. |
| **trivial** | Look up antonyms of *great* and of *important*. |
| **trot** | Look up *run*. |
| **trudge** | Look up *walk*. |
| **tug** | Look up *pull*. |
| **tumble** | Look up *fall*. |

# U & V

| | |
|---|---|
| **ugly** | Look up antonyms of *beautiful* and of *kind*. |
| **unafraid** | Look up antonyms of *afraid*. |
| **unattractive** | Look up antonyms of *beautiful*. |
| **unclean** | Look up antonyms of *clean*. |
| **uncover** | Look up *find*. |
| **unearth** | Look up *find*. |
| **uneven** | Look up *rough*.<br>Look up antonyms of *smooth*. |
| **unfasten** | Look up antonyms of *shut*. |
| **unfriendly** | Look up *cold*. |
| **unhappy** | Look up *sad*.<br>Look up antonyms of *happy*. |
| **unhurried** | Look up antonyms of *fast* (adj). |
| **unimportant** | Look up antonyms of *important*. |
| **uninteresting** | Look up antonyms of *interesting*. |
| **unjust** | Look up antonyms of *right*. |
| **unkind** | Look up antonyms of *kind*. |
| **unloaded** | Look up antonyms of *full*. |
| **unmask** | Look up antonyms of *hide*. |
| **unpleasant** | Look up antonyms of *kind*. |
| **unruffled** | Look up antonyms of *mad*. |
| **unsafe** | Look up *dangerous*. |
| **unspotted** | Look up *clean*.<br>Look up antonyms of *dirty*. |
| **unstained** | Look up *clean*. |

| | |
|---|---|
| **untidy** | Look up antonyms of *clean*. |
| **unusual** | Look up *queer*. |
| **uproar** | Look up *noise*. |
| **useful** | Look up *good*. |

A **vacant** chair is one with nobody sitting in it.

| | |
|---|---|
| **vacant** | Look up *empty*. <br> Look up antonyms of *full*. |
| **valuable** | Look up *good* and *important*. |
| **vanish** | Look up *go*. |
| **vast** | Look up *large*. |
| **vault** | Look up *jump*. |
| **velvety** | Look up *smooth*. |
| **view** | Look up *look*. |
| **virtually** | Look up *about*. |
| **vivid** | Look up *bright*. <br> Look up antonyms of *dim*. |
| **voyage** | Look up *trip* (n). |

# W

**walk**
step

*Walk* means move along on foot. You *step* when you raise your feet, one after the other, and put them down in another place. When you take steps, you are *walking*. When someone says, "*Step* lively!" that person wants you to *walk* faster. "*Step* this way," means that you are to follow.

march

*March* means walk steadily, with a regular step. Bands *march* by walking to the beat of drums.

stride

*Stride* means take long steps. A girl or boy might *stride* along to keep up with a taller person. Scott *strode* from the room.

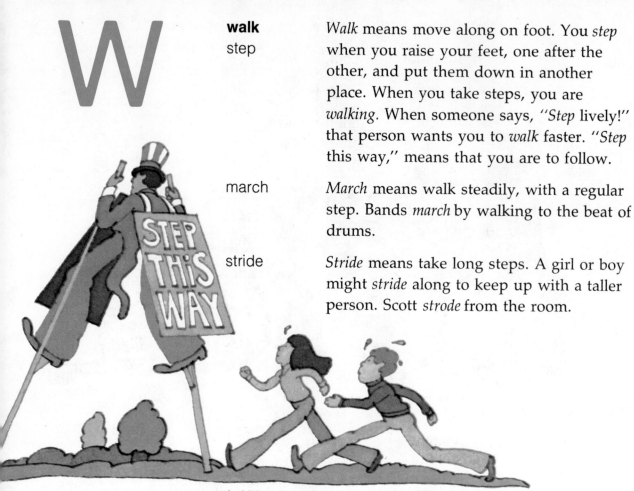

A child might **stride** to keep up with an older person.

tiptoe

*Tiptoe* means walk on your toes. Tom *tiptoed* through the room where the baby was sleeping.

stalk

*Stalk* means walk stiffly and perhaps angrily. Ann *stalked* out of the room. It can also mean walk cautiously when hunting — in order to follow or catch something. Cats *stalk* mice.

amble
saunter
stroll

*Amble, saunter,* and *stroll* mean walk easily and probably slowly, for fun. When you are out for a walk, you might decide to

214

*amble* over to a friend's house. You might *saunter* along a path in the park. People *stroll* on a warm summer evening.

**hike**

If you *hike*, you take a long walk for fun or for exercise. Scouts often *hike* through the woods and then make camp.

**clump**

*Clump* means walk noisily and clumsily. I used to *clump* around the house in a pair of Grandpa's old shoes.

**trudge**

*Trudge* means walk when walking is very hard. When she was young, Grandma had to *trudge* miles through the snow to school. People *trudge* through sand on the beach.

**shuffle**

*Shuffle* means walk without raising the feet. A very old person sometimes *shuffles* down the street. You would *shuffle* along if you thought your shoes might fall off.

**lurch**

Sometimes when you can't keep your balance, you *lurch* or roll to one side. We all *lurched* as the bus turned the corner.

**walk** continued on page 216 ▶

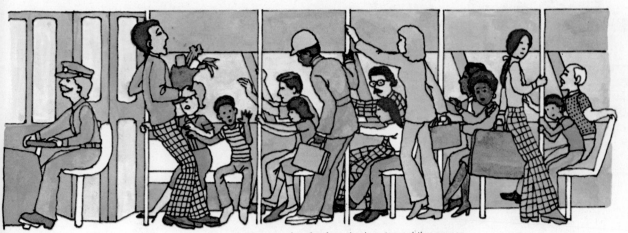

The passengers **lurched** as the bus turned the corner.

215

# W

| | |
|---|---|
| trip<br>stumble | *Trip* and *stumble* mean walk unsteadily because you have struck your foot against something. You might fall or you might continue walking. Ray *tripped* on the first step, then *stumbled* down the next five. |
| stagger | *Stagger* means move from side to side while walking. If you ride on a merry-go-round and get dizzy, you may *stagger* when you get off. |
| limp | *Limp* means walk unevenly by putting more weight on one leg than on the other. The runner *limped* over to the sidelines after twisting her ankle. |
| hobble | *Hobble* means move with difficulty, taking short steps. Sometimes a horse is hobbled—that is, its legs are roped together—to keep it from wandering away. You can imagine how much difficulty a horse would have walking that way, so it would *hobble*. |
| **want** | Look up *like*. |
| **war** | Look up *fight*. |
| **warm** | Look up *hot*.<br>Look up antonyms of *cold*. |
| **watch** | Look up *look*. |
| **watchful** | Look up antonyms of *careless*. |
| **watery** | Look up *wet*. |
| **weak** | Look up antonyms of *strong*. |
| **weird** | Look up *queer*. |
| **well-nigh** | Look up *about*. |

The movie about Mars had some **weird** creatures in it.

| | |
|---|---|
| **wet** | *Wet* means covered with water or not yet dry. A *wet* floor is usually slippery. The park bench had a sign on it that said "Wet Paint." The following words describe just how *wet* something is. |
| damp<br>moist | *Damp* and *moist* mean slightly wet. Use a *damp* cloth to wipe away the fingerprints. Your hair may feel *damp* after you take a shower. Just after a rainstorm the air feels *moist*. |
| soggy | *Soggy* means heavy with water or moisture. Bread gets *soggy* if it is covered with gravy. A swamp is *soggy*, but a desert is arid and dry. |
| soaking<br>drenched | *Soaking* and *drenched* mean completely wet. I tried to squeeze the water out of my *soaking* shirt. Before we got out of the rain, we were completely *drenched*. |
| watery | *Watery* means containing water. The soup didn't have much flavor; it was too *watery*. Land so dried out that it contains no water is parched. |
| rainy | *Rainy* means wet with lots of rain. On a *rainy* afternoon you must either play indoors or put on your raincoat and boots before going outside. |
| sloppy | *Sloppy* can mean wet enough to spatter and splash. When snow begins to melt, it becomes *sloppy*. Some sandwiches are called "Sloppy Joes" because they may splash when you eat them. |

Some sandwiches are called
"**Sloppy** Joes."

ANTONYMS: arid, dry, parched

**217**

Bloodhounds always look **woebegone.**

**whisper**  Look up antonyms of *shout.*

**wide**  Look up antonyms of *thin.*

**wild**  Look up antonyms of *quiet* (adj).

**win**  Look up *get.*

**wise**  Look up *smart* (adj).

**withdraw**  Look up antonyms of *put.*

**witty**  Look up *funny.*

**woebegone**  Look up *sad.*
Look up antonyms of *happy.*

**wonder**  Look up *think.*

**wonderful**  *Wonderful* is one of the most overworked words in our language. Originally *wonderful* and wondrous meant full of wonder or surprise. Now most people use *wonderful* for anything that is even slightly pleasing, exciting, remarkable, or good. They read a *wonderful* book, meet a *wonderful* person, have a *wonderful* trip, see a *wonderful* movie, or eat a *wonderful* piece of apple pie. How about trying some other words for *wonderful?*

pleasant
delightful
enjoyable  If something gives pleasure or joy, it is *pleasant, delightful,* or *enjoyable.* They spent a *pleasant* day. The puppet show was *delightful.* Ted had an *enjoyable* trip.

astonishing  If something is *astonishing,* it's so wonderful that it's amazing. The painting looked so real it was *astonishing.*

marvelous  If something is *marvelous,* it causes wonder or admiration. Gail has a *marvelous* voice.

wonderful continued

fabulous    If something is *fabulous,* it's too wonderful for the real world. It must have come out of a fable. Have you read the *fabulous* adventures of Ali Baba?

splendid    *Splendid* and *superb* mean unusually fine or
superb      excellent. She did a *splendid* job of making herself look like an old woman. We had expected to see a good movie, but this one was *superb.*

spectacular    Something *spectacular* is wonderful to look at. It makes a grand sight. The swimmer made a *spectacular* dive. The fireworks last night were truly *spectacular.*

You will find some more *wonderful* words that you may be able to use if you look up *beautiful, brave, bright, clean, funny, good, great, happy, important, interesting, kind, right, smart* (adj).

ANTONYMS: ordinary, plain

Some engines **work** by steam.

**work**    Look up *run.*

**wreck**    Look up *break.*
Look up antonyms of *make.*

**wretched**    Look up *sad.*
Look up antonyms of *happy.*

**wrinkled**    Look up antonyms of *smooth.*

**wrong**    Look up *bad.*
Look up antonyms of *right.*

# Y

**yell**      Look up *say* and *shout*.

**yodel**    Look up *shout*.

**young**   Look up antonyms of *old*.

People living in the mountains often **yodel.**

# SETS

special names
for groups of people, places, and things

When you think of a set of twins, you may picture two brothers or two sisters or a brother and sister. They were born about the same time, and perhaps they look so much alike that you can't tell them apart. When you think of a set of dishes, you may picture a number of plates and cups and saucers with the same pattern or color—enough to serve several people. You might think about sets of numbers every day in math class.

Sets of things are groups of things that have something in common. A set can be a group of things that grow together, like grapes or trees.

A set can be a family of animals that live together, like bees or kittens.

A set can be a group of people who work or play together or who are all interested in one thing, like a clean-up committee or a baseball team.

A set can be things that are put together or held in different ways, like sticks or hay.

A set can be things to ride in or on.

In our language there are many special words that have the same meaning as *set*. For example, the word *bunch* is used to describe a set of grapes.

The following pages contain names for different kinds of sets.

# Sets of Things

a **bundle** of sticks

a **cluster** of flowers

a **bunch** of grapes

a **bale** of hay

a **clump** of trees

## Sets of Animals

a **pack** of wolves

a **swarm** of bees

a **school** of dolphins

a **litter** of kittens

a **flock** of sheep

a **herd** of buffaloes

225

## Sets of Animals

a **skein** of geese

a **brood** of chicks

a **brace** of ducks

a **pride** of lions

a **pod** of seals

a **covey** of quail

a **gaggle** of geese

## Sets of People

a **class**

an **audience**

a **convention**

a **crowd**

## Sets of People

a baseball **team**

a police **force**

a **troop** of Girl Scouts

a clean-up **committee**

# Trains

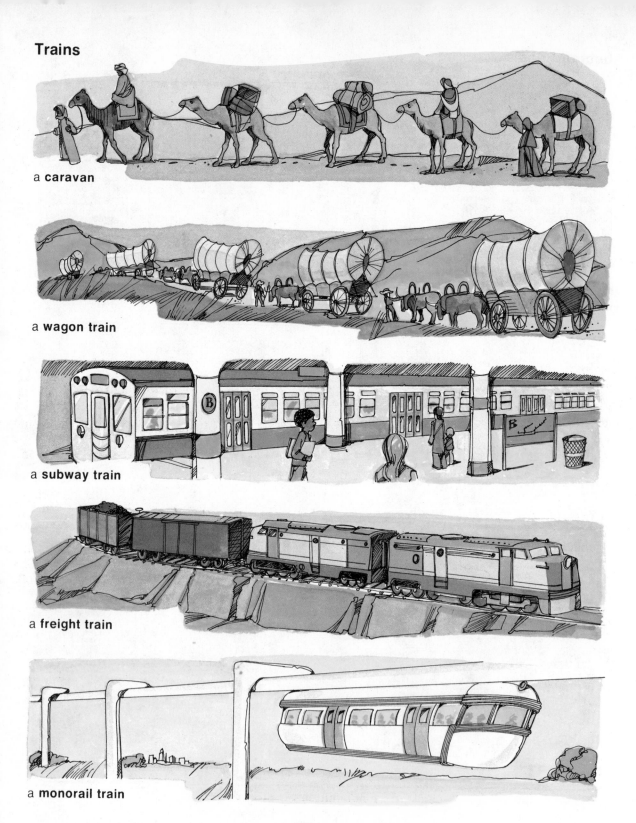

a caravan

a wagon train

a subway train

a freight train

a monorail train

# Aircraft

a **balloon**

a **glider**

a **blimp**

a **helicopter**

an **amphibian**

a **jet**

a **rocket**

231

# Boats

a **speedboat**

a **sailboat**

a **life raft**

a **canoe**

a **gondola**

a **kayak**

# Ships and Boats

a **Viking ship**

a **schooner**

a **submarine**

a **Yankee clipper ship**

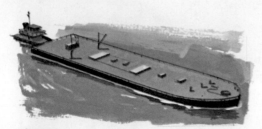

a **barge**

a **Chinese junk**

a **ferryboat**

## Bodies of Water

A **river** is a large stream of water.

A **brook** or **creek** is a small stream of water.

A **waterfall** is a body of water that continues to fall from a high place.

A **spring** is a small stream of water that comes up from the ground.

A **rapids** is a part of a river that moves very quickly, often over rocky land.

## Bodies of Water

A **lake** is a body of
water surrounded by land.

A **pond** is a body of water that is like a
lake, but much smaller.

A **puddle** is a small pool of water that is
often dirty.

A **swamp** or **marsh** looks like a body of
water, but it is really land that is kept wet
and soft by standing water.

A **water hole** is a hole in the ground
where water collects.

# Land Shapes

A **mesa** is a small piece of land with very steep sides and a flat top.

A **mountain** is a very, very large pile of earth materials like dirt and rocks.

A **cliff** is a very, very steep slope of rock.

A **knoll** is a small mound or pile of dirt.

A **hill** is a mound of dirt that is bigger than a knoll and smaller than a mountain.

## Land Shapes

A **canyon** is a narrow valley between mountains with very steep sides. Often there is a stream in the valley.

A **valley** is usually flat land at the bottom of hills or mountains.

A **gorge** is a narrow valley with steep, rocky sides.

A **ravine** is a small narrow valley with steep sides.

# Water Areas Near Land

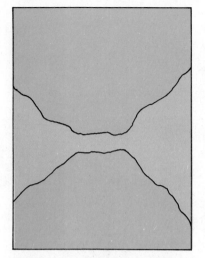

A **strait** is a narrow body of water that connects two larger bodies of water.

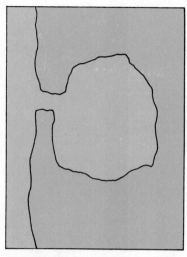

A **harbor** is an area of deep water near the shore. It is protected from strong winds and waves.

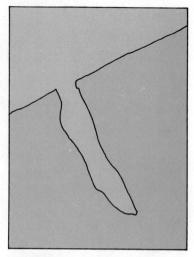

An **inlet** is a small body of water that moves into the land from a larger body of water.

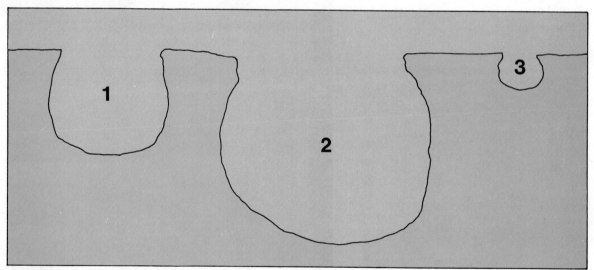

1. A **bay** is an area where water cuts into a shoreline.

2. A **gulf** is a large bay.

3. A **cove** is a small bay.

## Land Areas Near Water

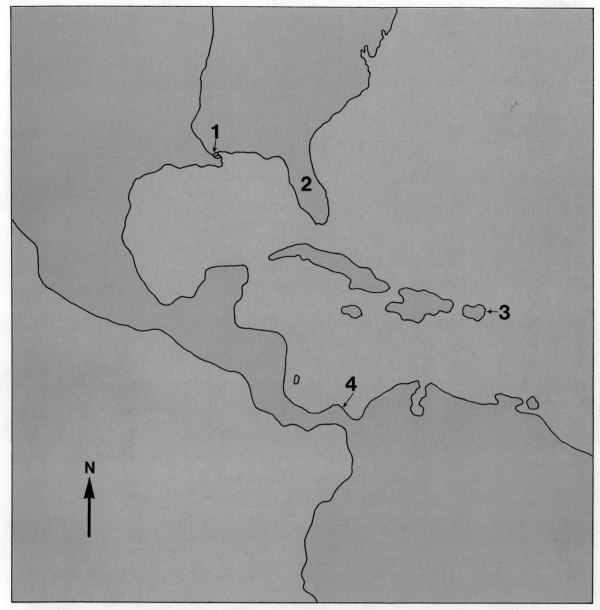

1. A **delta** is a piece of land built up from sand dropped near the mouth of a river. The Mississippi **delta** is in Louisiana.

2. A **peninsula** is land almost surrounded by water. Florida is a **peninsula.**

3. An **island** is land surrounded by water. Puerto Rico is an **island.**

4. An **isthmus** is a narrow strip of land that connects two larger areas of land. The **Isthmus** of Panama connects North America and South America.

Answers to questions on page 4–18.

## Exercises

### Reviewing the Parts (page 9)
A. The entry word is **mad**.
B. The entry is 3 pages long.
C. 8 synonyms are given for **noise**.
D. 4 antonyms are given for **hurry**.
E. *hot* and *cold*
F. adjective and adverb
G. *comical* and *hilarious*

### Choosing Synonyms (page 10)
A-1. faded
A-2. ramble
B-1. flushed
B-2. sultry
C-1. hauled
C-2. towing

### Choosing Antonyms (page 11)
A. happy
B. smooth
C. empty
D. easy
E. push

## Games

### The Good Game (page 12)
1-20. Answers will vary.

### The Action Game (page 14–15)
*Different words for* **jump**
1. hurdle or leap
2. vault
3. leap or hurdle
4. hop or bound
5. hurdle or leap over
Sentences will vary.
*Different words for* **run**
1. jog
2. lope
3. race or gallop
4. race or chase
5. sprint or race
Sentences will vary.

### The How Game (page 16)
Answers will vary.

### The Set Game (page 18)
Answers will vary.